CAMBRIDGE
Global English

for Cambridge Secondary 1
English as a Second Language

Coursebook

8

Michael

Chris Barker and Libby Mitchell

CAMBRIDGE
UNIVERSITY PRESS

CAMBRIDGE
UNIVERSITY PRESS

University Printing House, Cambridge CB2 8BS, United Kingdom

One Liberty Plaza, 20th Floor, New York, NY 10006, USA

477 Williamstown Road, Port Melbourne, VIC 3207, Australia

4843/24, 2nd Floor, Ansari Road, Daryaganj, Delhi – 110002, India

79 Anson Road, #06–04/06, Singapore 079906

Cambridge University Press is part of the University of Cambridge.

It furthers the University's mission by disseminating knowledge in the pursuit of education, learning and research at the highest international levels of excellence.

Information on this title: education.cambridge.org

© Cambridge University Press 2014

First published 2014
20 19 18 17 16 15 14 13

Printed in Spain by GraphyCems

A catalogue record for this publication is available from the British Library

ISBN: 978-1107-61942-5 Paperback

Cambridge University Press has no responsibility for the persistence or accuracy of URLs for external or third-party internet websites referred to in this publication, and does not guarantee that any content on such websites is, or will remain, accurate or appropriate. Information regarding prices, travel timetables, and other factual information given in this work is correct at the time of first printing but Cambridge University Press does not guarantee the accuracy of such information thereafter.

Welcome to Cambridge Global English Stage 8
for Cambridge Secondary 1 English as a Second Language

Cambridge Global English for Cambridge Secondary 1 English as a Second Language is a nine-stage course for learners of English as a Second Language (ESL). The nine stages range from the beginning of primary (Stages 1–6) to the end of junior secondary (Stages 7–9). It is ideal for all international ESL learners, and particularly for those following the Cambridge Primary/Secondary English as a Second Language Curriculum Framework, as it has been written to adhere to this framework. It presents realistic listening, speaking, reading and writing tasks, as well as end-of-unit projects similar to those students might encounter in the context of a first-language school. The course is organised into eighteen thematic units of study based on the Cambridge English ESL Scheme of work for Stage 8. After every other unit, there is a literature spread, featuring authentic prose, poetry, plays and songs from a variety of sources.

Cambridge Global English materials are aligned with the Common European Framework of Reference. The materials reflect the following principles:

- *An international focus.* Specifically developed for young learners throughout the world, the topics and situations in *Cambridge Global English* have been selected to reflect this diversity and encourage learning about each other's lives through the medium of English.

- *A cross-curricular, language-rich approach to learning. Cambridge Global English* engages learners actively and creatively. At the same time as participating in a range of curriculum-based activities, they practise English language and literacy and develop critical thinking skills.

- *English for educational success.* To meet the challenges of the future, learners will need to develop facility with both conversational and more formal English. From the earliest stage, *Cambridge Global English* addresses both these competencies. Emphasis is placed on developing the listening, speaking, reading and writing skills learners will need to be successful in using English-language classroom materials.

In addition to this Coursebook, *Cambridge Global English Workbook 8* provides supplementary support and practice. Comprehensive support for teachers is available in *Cambridge Global English Teacher's Resource 8.*

We hope that learners and teachers enjoy using *Cambridge Global English Stage 8* as much as we have enjoyed writing it.

Chris Barker and Libby Mitchell

Contents

	Reading/Topic	Listening/Speaking	Use of English	Vocabulary	Writing
Unit 5 **Sports and hobbies**	Sports and sports equipment Sporting ability An article about two top women athletes A web forum about hobbies	**Listening** Sports commentaries **Speaking** Ask and answer questions in a sports quiz Discuss what it takes to be a top sportsperson Talk about hobbies	Compound nouns (*ice hockey, goal post*) Abstract nouns (*strength, agility*) Present perfect continuous	Sports and sports equipment (*horse riding, reins, saddle*) Qualities associated with sport (*co-ordination, speed*) Hobbies (*judo, juggling, making model planes*)	Sentences using abstract nouns A web forum post about your hobbies
Project	A flyer for an after-school club				
Unit 6 **Entertainment and media**	Free time An article about the circus as a way of life A film review	**Listening** An informal and a formal way of talking about free-time activities A profile of the Cirque du Soleil **Speaking** Talk about free-time activities Discuss life in a circus and whether animals should be used in circuses Give your opinions of a film	Phrasal verbs: *take up, go out* Position of adverbs	Free-time activities (*playing the flute, doing taekwondo*) The circus and circus performers (*acrobat, circus ring*) Film reviews (*performance, script, soundtrack*)	A paragraph about free-time activities
Project **Fiction** **Review**	A film review *Bend it like Beckham* by Narinder Dhami Review of Units 5–6				
Unit 7 **Household routines**	Kitchen appliances and equipment A magazine article in which teenagers describe their bedrooms A quiz about jobs at home	**Listening** Typical kitchen conversations **Speaking** Talking about your room at home Ask and answer questions in a quiz and make comparisons	Phrasal verbs (kitchen and home): *put on, switch off, turn down* Compound nouns: *coffee machine, fire extinguisher* Compound adjectives for colours: *light blue* Comparative adjectives with *much, far … than, a lot less … than, just as … as, nowhere near as …. as*	Kitchen appliances and equipment (*dishwasher, iron*) Bedroom contents (*bedspread, noticeboard*)	A description of a room
Project	Design your own room				
Unit 8 **Habitat interactions**	Tropical rainforests Photosynthesis and aerobic respiration An article about a young inventor Food chains and the effect of habitat changes	**Listening** A nature documentary about rainforests A conversation about science homework An extract from a TV science programme **Speaking** Discuss the importance of rainforests, trees and plants for the environment Discuss the advantages and disadvantages of an invention to help farmers and wildlife in Kenya	Present passive Present perfect active and passive	Science: photosynthesis and aerobic respiration (*energy, glucose, oxygen*) The food chain (*predator, prey, herbivore*)	A tweet describing an invention A summary of how human activity can affect the food chain
Project **Fiction** **Review**	Animals and the food chain *The Whale Rider* by Witi Ihimaera Review of Units 7–8				

	Reading/Topic	Listening/Speaking	Use of English	Vocabulary	Writing
Unit 9 **Buildings and structures**	A general knowledge quiz about famous buildings and structures An article about the Millau Viaduct A new look at school design	**Listening** The answers to a general knowledge quiz **Speaking** Give a presentation about a bridge Talk about the design features of your school	Questions beginning with prepositions: *in which, for whom* Past continuous, active and passive	Buildings and structures (*palace, stadium, pyramid*) Bridges (*suspension bridge, viaduct*) Parts of a school (*classroom, staircase, storey*)	A fact file about a bridge
Project	Design your ideal school				
Unit 10 **Design and shape**	Shopping for food Three-dimensional shapes Classic designs	**Listening** A conversation about shopping for food A radio programme about the shapes of everyday objects Descriptions of classic designs **Speaking** Role-play a food shopping conversation Discuss everyday shapes Give your opinions about classic designs	Quantifiers with countable and uncountable nouns: *a bar of, a slice of*	Containers (*can, bottle*) Unit nouns (*loaf*) Group nouns (*bunch*) Shapes (*sphere, cube*) Adjectives to describe everyday objects (*simple, practical*)	A shopping list
Project **Poetry** **Review**	Design a product *Where I come from* by Elizabeth Brewster Review of Units 9–10				
Unit 11 **Personality types**	Aspects of personality A profile of a young inventor Soap opera	**Listening** A radio discussion about soap opera **Speaking** Talk about personality types Talk about a soap opera, the main characters, their personalities and the emotions that feature most frequently	Adjectives followed by prepositions: *interested in, good at* Prepositions followed by nouns: *at university, in the news* Abstract nouns: *jealousy, greed*	Personality adjectives (*calm, determined*) Abstract nouns and their corresponding adjectives to describe personality (*generosity, generous*)	A summary of a news story for a website
Project	A description of a soap opera				
Unit 12 **People and their jobs**	Jobs and places of work Talking about jobs A day in the life of a firefighter What you'll be doing in ten years' time	**Listening** Identify jobs from what people say about their work **Speaking** Talk about the people you know and the jobs they do Talk about the jobs you would like to do Talk about what you'll be doing in ten years' time and make suggestions for career choices	Suffixes for job titles (*dentist, receptionist, manager, plumber*) Verbs and prepositions followed by verb + -ing (*avoid doing, by checking*) *will* future and future continuous	Jobs (*optician, doctor*) The world of work (*duties, shift*)	A paragraph about the job you'd like to do
Project **Fiction** **Review**	A day in the life of someone doing a particular job *Rickshaw Girl* by Mitali Perkins Review of Units 11–12				
Unit 13 **Shops and services**	Supermarkets An article about the psychology of shopping in a supermarket Choosing a present and organising a celebration	**Listening** Supermarket announcements Plans for a celebration **Speaking** Describe a supermarket, what it has on offer and the layout Describe objects without saying their names	Prepositions followed by nouns (*on offer, at half price*) Reflexive pronouns (*help yourself, you can weigh them yourself*) Prepositions after adjectives and verbs (*afraid of, agree with*)	Supermarket (*trolley, checkout, bakery*)	Write a paragraph about the advantages and disadvantages of supermarkets
Project	Plan a celebration				

	Reading/Topic	Listening/Speaking	Use of English	Vocabulary	Writing
Unit 14 **Possessions and personal space**	A web forum about treasured possessions My room Adverts for buying and selling things	**Listening** An interview with a teenager about his room **Speaking** Use what people say about their treasured possessions to talk about personalities Talk about your own most treasured possessions Describe an object without giving its name Give your opinion about a room	*to have something done* Past perfect in reported speech Compound adjectives (*well-known*)	Personal possessions (*sports trophies, friendship bracelet*) Bedroom contents	A post for a web forum about treasured possessions A 'for sale' advert
Project **Autobiography** **Review**	Organise a charity sale *Coming to England* by Floella Benjamin Review Units 13–14				
Unit 15 **Natural disasters**	Natural disasters A report of a drought in East Africa Raising money for charity	**Listening** A news report about a natural disaster A conversation at a charity event **Speaking** Discuss the problems that are caused by drought	Present perfect active and passive *despite, in spite of* Modals: *can / can't, must / mustn't, have to / don't have to*	Natural disasters (*floods, hurricanes*) Games at a charity fête	Write an information leaflet for a charity
Project	Organise a school fête for charity				
Unit 16 **Survivors**	Disaster and survival An extract from a review of a book about a plane crash survivor An article about a mining disaster and a rescue Survival kits	**Listening** An extract from a radio book club programme **Speaking** Discuss three stories of survival Talk about what you need for a day's expedition	Comparative adverbs	Disasters and survivors (*explosion, survival instinct*) Survival kit (*whistle, water bottle. compass*)	A paragraph about a plane crash survivor
Project **Travel/** **Autobiography** **Review**	Plan a day's expedition *Touching the Void,* by Joe Simpson Review of Units 15–16				
Unit 17 **Summer season**	Summer holidays Summer camps and outdoor activities A summer camp in Japan Staying in a hostel	**Listening** Dialogues between a hostel manager and guests **Speaking** Give your opinions about the kind of summer holiday you like or don't like Compare summer camp schedules	Past modals: *should have, could have, would have* Indirect and embedded questions: *Could you tell me what time breakfast is, please? You need to tell me what time you want it.*	Summer holiday items (*insect repellent, sun cream*) Summer camp activities (*kayaking, mountain biking*)	A letter or message to a friend explaining why you wish they had come on a recent trip or holiday with you
Project	Write a comedy sketch set in a youth hostel				
Unit 18 **Using English**	Performing on stage The story of King Midas Writing and performing scenes from a play	**Listening** Two auditions for parts in a play **Speaking** Talk about performing in the theatre Talk about the story of Midas	Reported speech (revision): statements, questions and commands Punctuation: full stops and commas	The theatre (*stage manager, props, performers, narrator*)	Rewrite a paragraph putting in the correct punctuation
Project **Fiction** **Review**	Write and perform a play about King Midas *The Village by the Sea* by Anita Desai Review of Units 17–18				

- **Topics** Languages you speak; the languages of Papua New Guinea; the advantages of knowing languages
- **Use of English** Determiners: *neither*, *each/every*, *all*, *both*; conjunctions: *although*, *while*, *whereas*

My language, your language

- How many languages can you name? Where are they spoken?

Vocabulary

1 Read what these students say about the languages they speak. How many languages and how many countries are mentioned?

" I live in New Zealand, so I speak English. I can count to ten in Japanese, Spanish, German and French, and I can speak a bit of Maori, the native language of New Zealand. Neither of my parents speaks a foreign language. They wish they'd learned languages at school. "

" I'm from Java, in Indonesia. I'm bilingual. I speak Javanese at home and Indonesian at school, because all our lessons are in Indonesian. I'm learning English and Japanese, but I'm not fluent yet! "

" English is my second language because my native language is Welsh. Everyone in my family speaks Welsh. I think if people come to live in Wales, they should learn to speak Welsh, so that it doesn't become extinct. I speak some Italian, too, because my grandparents are Italian. Every time I go to visit them, I learn a bit more. "

" I live in Hong Kong. My mum speaks Mandarin Chinese and my dad speaks English, so I speak both these languages at home. At school our lessons are in Cantonese. I think each language has its own difficulties but the more languages you learn, the easier it gets. "

Did you know?

- About 7,000 different languages are spoken around the world.
- In Asia, there are 2,200 languages; in Europe, there are only 260.
- The world's most widely spoken languages are: Mandarin Chinese, English, Spanish, Hindi, Arabic, Bengali, Russian, Portuguese, Japanese, German and French.

In which countries are these languages spoken?

How many languages are spoken in your country?

2 Find a word or a phrase in the text in Exercise 1 which means the same as the following:

1 a little *a bit of*
2 the language of the country you were born in
3 speaking two languages
4 able to use a foreign language easily
5 the language you learn after your first language
6 no longer existing

Speaking

3 Work with a partner. Talk about the languages you speak.

- Choose one or two of the statements in Exercise 1 and adapt them so that they are true for you.

4 Complete the sentences with *all, both, neither, every*. Remember to use *of* where necessary.

1 <u>*Both (of)*</u> my parents speak English, so I hear it a lot at home.
2 I've got two English friends and _____ them are from London. They were born there.
3 My two cousins live in India, but _____ them has ever been to Mumbai.
4 I practise my Italian _____ summer when I go to see my grandparents in Bologna.
5 In English, _____ the words for languages start with a capital letter.

5 Work with a partner or in small groups. Think of your family and friends. Talk about the languages they speak.

> My grandparents live in ...
> Both of them speak ...
> Neither of them speaks ...

Use of English: Determiners: *neither, each/every, all, both*

Use *both (of)*, *neither of* to talk about two people or things.
My mum speaks Mandarin Chinese and my dad speaks English, so I speak both (of) these languages at home.
Neither of my parents speaks a foreign language.

Each and *every* have the same meaning, but *every* is more common than *each*.
Every / Each time I go to visit them, I learn a bit more.

Use *all* to talk about three or more people or things. Use *every* to talk about individual people and things. Use *all* with a plural verb and *every* with a singular verb.
All my lessons are in Indonesian.
Every lesson is in Indonesian.

You can use *the, my*, etc. after *all*, but not after *every*:
All my cousins speak Italian.
NOT *Every my cousins speak Italian.*

You must use *of* after *both, neither, each* and *all* before a pronoun:
both of us, neither of us, each of them, all of you

Teach yourself Tok Pisin!

- Before you read, look at the map and answer these questions.

1 Where exactly is Papua New Guinea? Use the following words in your answer: *north, east, in*.
2 What languages do you think are spoken in Papua New Guinea?

Reading

1 Read the text. What is the most surprising fact about Papua New Guinea?

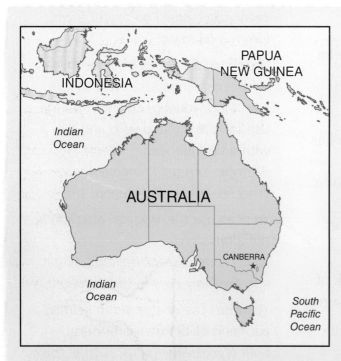

Papua New Guinea is the eastern part of the island of New Guinea. It has a population of just over seven million people. The capital is Port Moresby. The country became independent from Australia in 1975. There are about 800 languages in Papua New Guinea. That's more languages than in any other country in the world.

Papua New Guinea is a land of mountains and rainforests. Most communities are isolated and have little contact with each other or with the outside world. It's for this reason that so many different languages have developed.

The official languages of Papua New Guinea are Tok Pisin, English and Hiri Motu.

Although English is an official language, it is only spoken as a first language by a small percentage of the population.

Tok Pisin is spoken by most people. It is an English-based creole. The word 'tok' comes from the English word 'talk' and means *word* or *speech*. 'Pisin' means *pidgin*. A pidgin language is one which is a mixture of two other languages, whereas a creole is a pidgin language that has become the mother tongue of a community. Tok Pisin started as a pidgin language and became a creole language.

Although the majority of Tok Pisin vocabulary comes from English, it also includes words from German, Portuguese, Latin and a number of other languages, such as Tolai and Malay.

Tok Pisin is sometimes used in the first three years of primary school in Papua New Guinea, while English is used in secondary education.

2 Read the text again and complete the notes.

Country *Papua New Guinea*
Capital
Population
Official languages
Total number of languages
Languages used in education

3 Answer these questions.

1 Why do you think there are so many languages in Papua New Guinea?
2 What is Tok Pisin?
3 What is the difference between a first language and an official language?

4 Join these sentences using the conjunctions in italics.

- *although*
  1 My dad only spent a month in Australia. However, he learned a lot of English when he was there.

    Although my dad only spent a month in Australia, he learned a lot of English when he was there.
  2 Geography is his favourite subject. However, he didn't know where Papua New Guinea was.
  3 She speaks really good English. However, she's never been to an English-speaking country.
  4 I didn't do much revision. However, I got good marks in the test.

- *while / whereas*
  5 Some people are good at languages. Others find it very difficult to learn another language.

    Some people are good at languages, whereas others find it very difficult to learn another language.
  6 I prefer reading and writing. My friend likes speaking and working in groups.
  7 English is quite easy to learn in the early stages. French is quite difficult.
  8 Russian uses the Cyrillic alphabet (привет). Polish uses the Roman alphabet (cześć).

Listening 2

5 Work with a partner. How good are you at learning a new language?
Listen and practise the expressions in Tok Pisin.

Use of English: *although, while* and *whereas*

Although, while and *whereas* are conjunctions. They join clauses in a sentence.

Although is used to contrast two ideas. Read these sentences:
English is an official language. However, it is only spoken as a first language by a small percentage of the population.

You can join them together by using *although*:
Although English is an official language, it is only spoken as a first language by a small percentage of the population.

Whereas and *while* balance two contrasting ideas.
A pidgin language is one which is a mixture of two other languages, whereas/while a creole is a pidgin language that has become the mother tongue of a community.

Tok Pisin is sometimes used in the first three years of primary school, while/whereas English is used in secondary education.

It's good to learn languages

- Why is it good to learn another language?

Listening

1 You're going to hear some short interviews about knowing another language. What does each person focus on? Match the topics to the names.

1 Daniel   d meeting people socially

Names	Topics
1 Daniel	a work
2 Suzanne	b health
3 Elliot	c travel
4 Ayisha	d meeting people socially
5 Ben	e entertainment
6 Lisa	f education

2 Match the words from the interviews with the correct definitions.

1 at ease   a abilities to do something well
2 advantages   b facts that tell you something is true
3 improves   c makes better
4 evidence   d relaxed
5 skills   e the good points about something

3 Listen again and answer these questions.

1 Why does Daniel think people are more willing to talk about themselves in their own language?
Because they are ...

2 According to Suzanne, what 'makes all the difference' when you visit another country?
Being able to ...

3 Why does Elliot like learning Spanish?
Because he can ...

4 Why is learning a language good for you, according to Ayisha?
Because it improves ...

5 What does Ben say about students who know another language?
They have better ...

6 According to Lisa, there are two advantages to knowing languages in the business world. What are they?
The first is that you're more likely to be .... The second is that you ...

4 Listen to the interviews again. Put your hand up when you hear each of these words and phrases.

1 definitely
2 even if
3 it's really useful

4 it makes all the difference
5 a little bit

6 of course
7 more likely to be
8 for example

Speaking

5 Work in groups. Give your views about the advantages of learning other languages. Try to use some of the words and phrases in Exercises 2 and 4.

Project: A mobile phone app

6 Design a mobile phone app to help you and other students learn English.

Work in groups. Decide what features it should have. Here are some ideas to help you. You can:

- look up the meaning of a word.
- watch films and cartoons in English.
- play games to practise your English.
- type in a word or sentence in your own language and see the translation.
- read short stories in English.
- listen to songs and see the words.
- hear the correct pronunciation of words or phrases.
- listen to a phrase. Then say it and record it. Compare and correct your pronunciation.
- learn grammar rules by watching animations.

Present your app to the class. Give examples to illustrate the features.

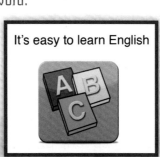

My mobile phone

With this mobile phone app you can do lots of things. You can:

- look up the meaning of a word.

You just type the word in and you can see the meaning.

It's easy to learn English

You can also:

2 E-communication

- **Topics** Using electronic communication; the School of the Air; schools of the future; advantages and disadvantages of email; email and mobile phone etiquette
- **Use of English** *to, in order to, so that, so as* to express purpose; *will* future, passive form; *wish (that), if only* + past perfect; *should have / shouldn't have*

Are you a good communicator?

- What are the advantages of mobile phones? Are there any disadvantages?

Speaking

1 Work in pairs. Think of someone you know who likes technology. Talk about the person using the prompts.

A *My brother likes technology. He uses a smartphone, a laptop and an iPod.*

B *What does he use them for?*

A *He uses the smartphone ...*

to make and receive calls / to send and receive texts / for work / to do homework / to access the Internet / to send and receive emails / to download apps / for social networking

Reading

2 Laura loves all kinds of new technology. David doesn't. Read the opinions. Which are Laura's and which are David's?

1 Although I've got an iPad, I still prefer the feel of a real book. *David*
2 Having access to the Internet means that you can look things up easily when you're doing your homework.
3 I don't think it's fair to download music for free. I like CDs.
4 I've got an app for learning Spanish. It's really useful.
5 When I'm meeting someone, I always take my mobile with me, so that I can call them if I'm running late.
6 It's so easy to keep in touch with your friends now through social networking.
7 Lots of my friends have blogs. Where do they find the time to write them?
8 Some people I know wouldn't go on holiday to a place without wi-fi. I think it's great to be somewhere with no wi-fi and where there's no mobile signal.
9 There's so much music you can download. It's much easier than buying CDs.
10 Why do people have to chat for so long on mobile phones when they're on a train or a bus?

Speaking

3 Work in pairs. Who gives the most convincing reasons, David or Laura?

4 What are these words and phrases in your language?

1 app
2 blog
3 Internet access
4 wi-fi
5 signal
6 to download
7 social networking

5 Match the two halves of each sentence and join them using *to, so that* or *so as*.

1 You can download apps
2 I always take my mobile phone with me when I go out
3 I use my iPod with headphones
4 I sent you a text
5 You need to turn off the alarm on your mobile
6 I've sent you my email address

a ask if you wanted to go to the cinema.
b help you learn a language.
c I can call my parents to tell them where I am.
d it doesn't wake you up at 5am!
e not to disturb Mum and Dad.
f you can get in touch with me.

1 You can download apps to help you learn a language.

Use of English: *to, in order to, so that* and *so as*

To express purpose, use these phrases.

Positive	
I went to the shop	*in order to have a look at the latest smartphones.* (formal)
	to have a look at the latest smartphones.
	so that I could have a look at the latest smartphones.

Negative	
I've switched my phone to 'Silent'	*in order not to disturb you.* (formal)
	so as not to disturb you.
	so that it doesn't disturb you.

Writing

6 Are you like Laura or like David from Exercise 2? Write a short paragraph giving your views about the gadgets in Exercise 1. Include some of the phrases from Exercises 1 and 2.

A mobile phone is really useful because ...

The future of schools

- How is your school today different from the school your parents went to?

Reading

1 Read this article about the School of the Air. What is it, and how is it different from a normal school?

Going to school is normal for Australian children who live near big cities and towns. However, some children live on farms in the outback, a long way from the nearest school. Thanks to the School of the Air, they are still able to get an education. How does it work?

Lessons are given by a teacher who is in a studio. The lessons are sent to the students by satellite, so that they can access them on their computers. They take part in the lessons in real time using a webcam.

"Hi! I'm Jane. I live on a cattle farm in Western Australia. I do all my lessons on my laptop at home. I have four lessons a day. There's a webcam and a microphone on the computer, so that I can talk to the teacher and other students. The teacher uses an interactive whiteboard in the studio, so we can type in our answers to the questions, which is fun. I send my homework by email. We all have a chance to meet at sports day which happens once a year. I'm really looking forward to it."

Perhaps the School of the Air is showing how education will work in the future, not just for children who live in remote areas but for all of us. Perhaps students will work from home and lessons will be given over the Internet. Schools with classrooms, libraries, music rooms and science laboratories won't be needed. And you'll have no excuse for being late for school!

Speaking

2 Work with a partner. Talk about the advantages and disadvantages of learning with the School of the Air.

3 Find the words in the text for the following:

1 A place where TV programmes, films and recordings are made.

2 A piece of equipment that is sent into space to travel around the earth in order to receive and send information.

3 A camera which records moving pictures and sound, so that they can be shown on the Internet as they happen.

4 A small computer that you can carry with you.

5 A piece of equipment for recording sound, so that it can be sent electronically.

6 A large electronic white screen which is used by teachers and students in a classroom.

4 Write a heading for each paragraph of the article.

Paragraph 1: Going to school in Australia

5 Write out the sentences using the *will* future passive form of the verbs in brackets.

1 Cars *won't be driven* by people; they _____ by computers. (*not drive, control*)

2 Text messaging _____ by voice-to-text technology. (*replace*)

3 All houses _____ by solar power. (*heat*)

4 There will be no shops or shopping centres. All shopping _____ online. (*do*)

5 Films _____ at cinemas. They _____ and _____ at home. (*not show, download, watch*)

Use of English: *will* future, passive form

Use the *will* passive to talk about what will be done in the future or to predict what you think will happen.

Positive

will be	+	past participle

Lessons will be given over the Internet.

Negative

(Remember that *will not* is often shortened to *won't*.)

Schools with classrooms, libraries, music rooms and science laboratories won't be needed.

Questions

Will all exams be taken online?

Discussion

6 **What will schools be like 20 years from now?**

1 Which of the following do you think will happen?

a There will be no schools. Students will work from home and all lessons will be given over the Internet.

b Teachers will be replaced by computers.

c Books will no longer exist. Everything will be downloaded from the Internet.

d Exams and tests will be taken online.

e Homework will not be handwritten. It will be done on the computer and it will be marked by a computer.

f Activities such as music, drama and sports won't be done in schools. They will be organised in the local communities.

2 What other changes do you think there will be?

3 What will students miss if they only learn from home and don't go to school?

I wish I hadn't done that!

- 'I wish I hadn't done that.' When might you think or say this?

Reading

1 Work with a partner. Read the cartoon. What's the story behind the pictures? What do you think has happened? Write down your ideas. Compare them in small groups.

2 Rewrite the following sentences using the prompts.

1 I've eaten too much.
I wish *I hadn't eaten so much*.

2 I didn't do enough revision for the exam.
If only _____ .

3 I didn't bring my camera.
I wish _____ .

4 You shook the bottle before you opened it. That was silly.
You shouldn't *have shaken the bottle before you opened it.*

5 I didn't bring a book to read. Now I'm bored.
I should _____ .

6 You didn't take a jacket to school. That's why you were cold.
You should _____ .

Use of English: *wish (that), if only* + past perfect; *should have / shouldn't have*

Use *I wish* + past perfect or *If only* + past perfect to express regret about something you've done.

I wish I hadn't sent that email.

If only I hadn't sent that email.

You can also use *should have* + past participle to express self-criticism or criticism of others.

I should have waited. I shouldn't have sent that email.

You should have phoned me. You shouldn't have sent that email.

3 Think about things you wish you'd done or hadn't done, and things you should have done or shouldn't have done. Write a list. Then tell your partner.

| I wish I had ... | I wish I hadn't ... | I should have ... | I shouldn't have ... |

> phoned my grandma last weekend

FAMILY

> been in a bad mood this morning

FRIENDS

> played better in the match

SPORTS & FREE TIME

> been late for the first lesson

SCHOOL

Listening (4)

4 When do people prefer to send an email rather than send a text? Before you listen, share your ideas with other students.

5 Listen to people talking about email. What is the conclusion? Do you agree with it?

6 Listen again. Makes notes on the advantages and disadvantages the students talk about. Compare your notes with a partner. Did you write down the same things?

Project: Email and mobile phone etiquette

(handwritten: etiket)

7 Work with a partner. Read this guide to email etiquette. Do you agree? Is there anything you would add?

- Do not use capitals letters. It's like SHOUTING when you're talking to somebody.
- Always check your emails before you send them. Make sure the spelling, grammar and punctuation are correct.
- Be careful what you write. Don't be rude. Don't say anything bad about other people – your email could be forwarded to them.
- Before you write an email, ask yourself: *Would a phone call be better?*

8 Work in groups. You're going to write a guide to mobile phone etiquette. Discuss your ideas and make notes. Think about:

- when and where it's <u>not</u> OK to use a mobile (during a meal, at the cinema, on public transport)
- responding to text and voice messages
- using the 'silent' mode
- leaving a message.

9 Now write the guide using your notes.

Enjoy your new phone!

Please take time to read this guide to mobile phone etiquette

Fiction

Isabel Allende is from Chile. Her book *City of the Beasts* is the first in a three-part series for young adults.

1 Look at the cover of the book on page 21. What sort of book do you think it is? What do you think it is about?

2 Read the summary of the story so far and the extract from Chapter 1. How does Alex feel?

3 Match the words and phrases to the definitions.

1 ship me off
2 package
3 furious
4 fist
5 documentary
6 mosquitoes
7 caimans
8 bandits
9 leprosy
10 piranhas

a people who rob travellers
b a film or TV programme that gives the facts about a situation
c send me somewhere (when I don't want to go there)
d a hand which is tightly closed
e something that is covered in paper and sent in the post
f a very serious disease which destroys the body
g South American fish with sharp teeth
h very angry
i insects that suck blood, sometimes causing malaria
j reptiles that are like small alligators

4 Find five words the author uses instead of *said*.

1 (his father) explained

5 Complete the family tree.

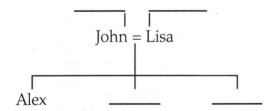

Alex

6 What does this extract tell you about the following characters?

1 Alex   2 Alex's father   3 Kate

7 Work in groups. Discuss these questions.

1 Alex says, *"I'm fifteen, Dad, and that's plenty old enough for you to at least ask my opinion."* Is he right?
2 What do you think is going to happen next in the story?

The story so far

Alex's mother, Lisa, is very ill. His father, John, is going to take her from their home in California to a hospital in Texas for some special treatment. This means that the family can't stay together. Alex is so upset and angry that he has smashed things in his room, cutting his hand.

City of the Beasts

"What will happen to the girls and me?"

"Andrea and Nicole will go live with their grandmother Carla. You are going to go to my mother," his father explained.

"Kate? I don't want to go to her, Dad! Why can't I go with my sisters? At least grandmother Carla knows how to cook."

"Three children would be too much for her."

"I'm fifteen, Dad, and that's plenty old enough for you to at least ask my opinion. It isn't <u>fair</u> for you to <u>ship me off to Kate</u> as if I were some <u>package</u> or something. That's always how it is. You make the decisions and I have to follow them. I'm not a baby any more!" Alex <u>protested</u>. He was <u>furious.</u>

"Well, sometimes you act like one." John smiled and pointed to the injured hand.

"It was an accident, it could have happened to anyone. I'll <u>behave</u> at Carla's, I promise."

"I know your <u>intentions</u> are good, son, but sometimes you act without thinking."

'I told you, I'll pay for everything I broke," <u>yelled</u> Alex, <u>banging</u> a fist on the table.

"You see how you can't control your <u>temper</u>? In any case, Alex, this has nothing to do with what you did to your room. Things were already <u>arranged</u> with Lisa's mother and mine. The three of you will have to go stay with your grandmothers; there's no other <u>solution</u>. You'll be leaving for New York in a couple of days," his father said.

"Alone?"

"Alone. I'm afraid that from here on you will have to do a lot of things alone. Take your <u>passport</u>, because I think you're going on an adventure with my mother."

"Where?"

"To the Amazon."

"The Amazon!" Alex <u>exclaimed, horrified</u>. "I saw a documentary about the Amazon. That place is <u>crawling</u> with mosquitoes and <u>caimans</u> and <u>bandits</u>. There are a million diseases there – even <u>leprosy</u>!"

"I expect that my mother knows what she's doing; she wouldn't take you anywhere you'd be in danger, Alexander."

"Kate is quite capable of pushing me into a river filled with <u>piranhas</u>," Alex blurted out. "With a grandmother like mine, I don't need <u>enemies</u>."

From *City of the Beasts* by Isabel Allende, HarperCollins 2002

Review of Units 1–2

Vocabulary

Languages

1 Complete these languages.

1 Arab _ic_
2 Japan___
3 Span___
4 Germ___
5 Chin___
6 Russ___

2 Complete the sentences with the words from the box.

> bilingual fluent native official second

1 I was born in Brazil, so Portuguese is my ____ language.
2 I grew up speaking two languages, Chinese and English. I hope being ____ will be an advantage for getting a job.
3 I speak English quite well, but I'm not ____.
4 Canada has two ____ languages: French and English.
5 Arabic is our first language, but a lot of people in my country speak French as a ____ language.

Use of English

3 Choose the correct word.

1 I've got six cousins. They *all / every* live in other countries, so I don't see them very much.
2 *Both / Each* my parents are bilingual. They speak Swahili and English.
3 Our teacher tries to give *each / all* student a chance to speak in our English lessons.
4 *Neither / Every* of my parents is as good at texting as I am.
5 *All / Every* the students in my class like working with the interactive whiteboard.

4 Match the two halves of the sentences.

1 Although our school is quite old,
2 My brother isn't good at languages,
3 At our school we learn English and Japanese,
4 Although some children in Australia live in the outback,
5 I like reading books on an e-reader,
6 Although I live ten kilometres from school,

a whereas my mum prefers real books.
b the journey only takes twenty minutes.
c it's got a modern Science block and a new gym.
d whereas he's brilliant at Maths and Science.
e while at my sister's school they learn English, Chinese or Russian.
f they can learn at home using a computer and a satellite connection.

5 Complete the sentences with *so as, so that, to / in order to*.

1 We sometimes work in groups, _so that_ we can share our ideas.
2 You can use the Internet __ find out things when you're doing a project.
3 Take your mobile __ you can phone me when you're ready to come home.
4 You need to study for at least five years __ become a doctor.
5 Let's do our homework now __ we can watch the match on TV later.
6 Our teacher asked us to be quiet __ not to disturb the students doing the exam in the next classroom.

6 Complete the details using the *will* future, passive form.

School trip: information for parents

1 Students *will be taken* to the activity centre by coach. *(take)*
2 Students __ a plan of the day's activities when they arrive. *(give)*
3 Lunch __. *(provide)*
4 Students __ at all times by a teacher. *(accompany)*
5 All the activities __ by qualified instructors. *(organise)*
6 Students __ to use mobile phones during the day. *(not allow)*

7 Complete what these people are saying in two ways. Use *wish (that),* *if only, should have* or *shouldn't have.*

1 My friends wanted me to go for a picnic at the weekend, but I didn't go. They had a really good time.
(I / go) *I wish I'd gone.*
I should have gone.
2 I feel so tired this morning.
(I / stay up so late)
3 Oh dear, I can't answer any of the questions in this test!
(I / do more revision)
4 I got into trouble for being late for school.
(I / get up earlier)
5 It was meant to be a surprise and now everybody knows, thanks to you!
(you / tell everybody)

General knowledge quiz

8 Work with a partner. Ask and answer the questions.

1 What is the native language of New Zealand?
2 What is Welsh?
3 How many different languages are there in the world?
 a about 700
 b about 7,000
 c about 70,000
4 There are far more languages spoken in Asia than in Europe. True or false?
5 What is the capital of Papua New Guinea?
6 What are the names of the two English-speaking countries on the map, south of Papua New Guinea?

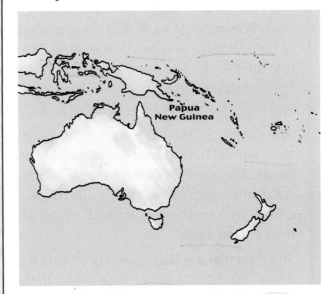

7 How many languages are spoken in Papua New Guinea?
8 привет This means 'hello'. Which language is it and what's the name of the alphabet used in this language?
9 What is the 'outback' in Australia?
10 Who studies at The School of the Air?

3 Rivers and coasts

- **Topics** The Nile and the ancient Egyptians; the water cycle; the Amazon river and rainforest; Robinson Crusoe Island
- **Use of English** Non-defining and defining relative clauses

The Nile

- Why are rivers important to people?

Reading

1 Read the text. Then tell your partner three things you have learned about the River Nile.

The Nile

The Nile is the longest river in the world. It flows from south to north and it has one source at Lake Victoria, in Uganda (the White Nile), and another at Lake Tana, in Ethiopia (the Blue Nile). In total it is 6,670 kilometres long.

The ancient Egyptians called the river *Ar* or *Aur*, meaning 'black', because of the black sediment left behind after the frequent river floods. The ancient Greeks called the river *Kem*, which also means 'black'. The name *Nile* comes from another Greek word, *neilos*, which means 'river valley'.

The area that the Nile covers is so vast that it has several different climate areas. In the north, in Egypt and Sudan, there is very little rain. Further south, in and around Ethiopia, rainfall is heavy, so this keeps the river

flowing, eventually creating the very fertile soil in Egypt and north Sudan. There are dams, such as the one at Aswan, which have been built across the river to prevent flooding in populated areas along the banks of the Nile.

The Nile delta, in northern Egypt, is where the river spreads out and flows into the Mediterranean Sea. From north to south, the delta is about 160 kilometres long. From west to east, it covers about 240 kilometres of coastline. It begins just down river from Cairo.

The Mediterranean Sea doesn't have a strong tide, but it is enough to bring salt water into the Nile's estuaries to mix with the river's fresh water. In the marshes and lagoons there are salt water crocodiles, the biggest living reptiles in the world.

24

2 Find a word in the text for each of the following definitions.

1 the place where a river starts   *source*
2 a layer of mud, sand, stones, etc. that forms at the bottom of a river
3 strong walls built across a river to stop the water
4 a low flat area of land where a river divides into smaller rivers and flows into the sea
5 the regular rise and fall in the level of the sea
6 the wide parts of rivers where they go into the sea
7 areas of soft, wet land
8 lakes that contain sea water

Listening 5

3 You're going to listen to an extract from a documentary about the Nile and the ancient Egyptians. Why do you think the Nile was important to them? Discuss your ideas as a class. Then listen and check.

4 Listen again and answer these questions.

1 In ancient times, when did the river flood?
2 How were the floods useful for farmers?
3 What was grown on the banks of the Nile?
4 What is *flax*? What is *papyrus*?
   Why was the Nile a useful defence against enemies?
   In what other way was the Nile useful to the ancient Egyptians?

Writing

5 Write a summary, in four paragraphs, of the extract from the documentary. The first paragraph has been done for you.

Four ways in which the Nile was important for the ancient Egyptians

food	The Nile was a source of food. Fish was the main source of animal protein for most people. Cereals, fruit and vegetables were grown on the banks of the Nile.
flax, papyrus	
defence	
transport	

Choose a caption for the photo or invent your own.
Is this my best side?
I'm ready for my close-up.
The salt water in these lagoons is so good for the skin.

The water cycle

- **Why do we need water?**

1 Match each of the following captions to a number on the water cycle diagram.

<u>Relief rainfall</u>

Water on the earth is constantly moving. It is recycled over and over again. This recycling process is called 'the water cycle'.

a Run off

Rain water and melted snow is taken by rivers back to the sea. The cycle starts again.

b Condensation – water vapour condenses into clouds

The water vapour is cooled as it rises and is changed back into tiny drops of liquid water, forming clouds.

c Evaporation – water evaporates into the air

The water in rivers, lakes and seas is heated by the sun and it turns into water vapour. The water vapour rises into the air.

d Wind

Clouds are blown inland by the wind.

e Precipitation – water falls as rain

Clouds get heavy and water falls back to the earth as rain or snow.

2 Read the text below and answer the questions.

1 Why is it always warm in the Amazon rainforest? (Think of where it is.)
2 What is the difference between 'convectional rainfall' and rainfall as shown in the water cycle diagram ('relief rainfall')?

The Amazon River Basin, which lies just below the equator, covers about 40% of South America. The Amazon Rainforest, which spreads out from the river, has rain almost every day of the year. It is hot and humid, with an average temperature of 27 degrees all year round. Moist air near the ground is heated, which causes it to rise. As it rises, it condenses and forms rain clouds. This is called 'convectional rainfall'.

Use of English: Relative clauses – non-defining

Relative clauses begin with a word like *who*, *which* or *that*. Non-defining relative clauses give extra information in a sentence.

Which often refers to a noun …

The Amazon River Basin, which lies just below the equator, covers about 40% of South America.

… but it can also refer to a whole clause.

Moist air near the ground is heated, which causes it to rise.

3 **Combine these sentences, using** *which*.

1 The Ganges opens into the Indian Ocean. It flows through India and Bangladesh.

The Ganges, which flows through India and Bangladesh, opens into the Indian Ocean.

2 The Amazon flows through six countries in South America. It is the second longest river in the world.

3 The Yangtze River is the third largest river in the world. It has its source in the snow-capped mountains of western China.

4 The Iguazu Falls can be seen from three countries. They're on the border between Argentina and Brazil.

5 We saw Niagara Falls from the plane. It was amazing.

We saw Niagara Falls from the plane, which was amazing.

6 It didn't rain on the day we went up the Amazon in a boat. It was very unusual.

7 The Amazon is very wide. This is why there were no bridges across it until recently.

8 Our flight was delayed for a day. It meant we could spend another day on the beach in Rio.

9 The river in our village often floods. This makes it difficult to get to school.

Speaking

4 **Work in small groups. Talk about a trip you've been on. Try to include some clauses starting with** *which*.

which was really interesting
which was very exciting
which was good fun
which I hadn't seen/done before

> Last month we went on a school trip to …, which was really interesting.

Writing

5 **Write an account of the trip you went on. Ask your partner to comment on it and correct it. Then write a final version.**

Saved by the bell!

- What is a tsunami?

Reading

1 Look at the text below. What does it describe?

Language tip

Note the use of prepositions to describe places:

off the coast **of** Chile

on the island

12-year-old girl saves islanders from tsunami

Robinson Crusoe is the largest of the islands which make up the Juan Fernández Archipelago, off the coast of Chile.

At 6am on Saturday 27th February 2010 in San Juan Bautista, the island's only town,

12-year-old Martina Maturana felt an earth tremor. She looked out of the window and noticed that the fishing boats in the harbour were bobbing up and down and crashing into each other. She immediately ran 400 metres from her home to the town square to ring the emergency bell. It was Martina's quick thinking which saved the lives of the majority of the 650 islanders. People ran to high ground for safety, escaping the massive wave that was caused by an earthquake off the coast of Chile. A few minutes later, a wall of water crashed onto the land and swept 300 metres into the village. The houses and buildings on the island that were close to the coast were immediately destroyed, including the school at which Martina was a student. "The wave was 20 metres high," said one man whose house was destroyed by the sea. "It was terrifying."

2 Read these three tweets about the story in Exercise 1. Which is best? Give reasons for your choice.

	X
1 A tsunami hit an island near Chile. Most people survived because a girl rang the emergency bell. Most houses and buildings were destroyed.	
2 Most people but not buildings survived a tsunami on Robinson Crusoe Island near Chile, thanks to a girl of 12 who rang the emergency bell.	
3 A tsunami hit Robinson Crusoe Island near Chile. A girl rang the emergency bell, people ran to safety. Houses and buildings were destroyed.	

Use of English: Relative clauses – defining

Defining relative clauses define exactly what you're talking about.

Robinson Crusoe is the largest of the islands which make up the Juan Fernández Archipelago.

People ran to high ground for safety, escaping the massive wave that was caused by an earthquake off the coast of Chile.

Notice that you can also use prepositions before *which*:

... including the school at which Martina was a student.

3 Find two more examples of defining relative clauses in the text in Exercise 1.

4 Add the sentences in column 2 to the questions in column 1 using *which/that*.

What's the name of the island which / that is off the south coast of Australia?

1 What's the name of the island?
2 What's the name of the city in Chile?
3 What's the name of the river?
4 When were the earthquake and tsunami?
5 What's the name of the crocodile?
6 What's the name of the sea?

a It runs through Paris, in France.
b They destroyed Lisbon, the capital of Portugal.
c It's off the south coast of Australia.
d It's the nearest to the Juan Fernández Archipelago.
e It's the world's largest reptile.
f It's between the north of Africa and the south of Europe.

Project: The Amazon river

5 Work in groups. You're going to collect information and illustrations for a magazine article about the Amazon or any major river of your choice (similar to the one on the Nile on page 24).

1 Start by deciding who is going to do each task.
2 Find information to complete a fact file.

3 Use the completed fact file to write your article.
4 Decide where the pictures and maps should go. Remember to label and caption them.

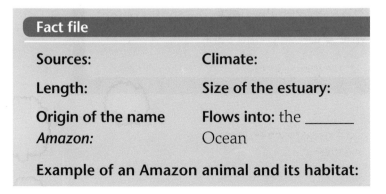

Fact file	
Sources:	Climate:
Length:	Size of the estuary:
Origin of the name *Amazon*:	Flows into: the _____ Ocean
Example of an Amazon animal and its habitat:	

4 Great expeditions

- **Topics** The sinking of the *Titanic* and exploration of the wreck; expeditions from China in the 15th century; space exploration
- **Use of English** Revision of past tenses; sentence adverbs *though* and *as well*; revision of the *will* future

Titanic

- Are you a traveller or do you prefer to stay near home? How would you feel about going on a long journey by sea?

Reading and listening 6

1 Read the text and number the paragraphs in the correct order. Then listen and check.

---

a However, by the following morning it was clear that more than 1,500 people had died and that only about 700 passengers had survived.

b It was making good progress across the Atlantic when, on the night of Sunday 14th April, five days after setting out, it hit an iceberg. A telegram was sent saying: "We have struck an iceberg."

c On Tuesday 16th April, the headlines in the newspapers read: "*Titanic* sunk, no lives lost" and "All *Titanic* passengers are safe".

d The ship went down within three hours of hitting the iceberg. It sank nearly four kilometres, to the bottom of the ocean. Some passengers managed to escape, but there weren't enough lifeboats to save everyone.

e *Titanic* was the biggest, fastest and most luxurious liner of its time. In April 1912, the ship set sail on its maiden voyage from Southampton in Great Britain to New York.

f While the passengers in the lifeboats were desperately trying to survive the freezing temperatures, the nearest ship, the *Carpathia*, had answered *Titanic*'s call for help and was heading at full speed to rescue them. It took the *Carpathia* four hours to reach the place where the ship had sunk.

2 Answer these questions.

1 What was the *Titanic*?
2 When did it set sail on its maiden voyage?
3 Where was it sailing from and to?
4 Why did the ship sink?
5 How long did it take for the *Titanic* to sink?
6 Why didn't all the passengers manage to escape?
7 What was the *Carpathia* and what part did it play in the story?
8 When did the world learn the truth abut the *Titanic*?

Speaking

3 Work in pairs. Use the answers to the questions in Exercise 2 to tell the story of the *Titanic* in your own words. Remember to use the correct past tense.

Listening ⑦

4 Listen to this radio discussion. The topic is: 'Exploring the wreck of the *Titanic* – is it right or wrong?' What do you think you're going to hear? Discuss your ideas as a class. Then listen and check.

5 Listen again and answer the questions.

1 How would you summarise Joe's view, Tania's view and Patrick's view about exploring the wreck and bringing back objects from it?

Joe thinks that it's all right to explore the wreck because it brings the story to life and helps you understand it.

2 What's Patrick's view on Adventure Tourism and people visiting the wreck?

3 What do Joe and Tania think about the wedding that took place on the deck of the *Titanic*?

Speaking

6 Work in groups. Continue the radio discussion. One of you is the presenter. Ask the guests the question. They give their own views.

> What do you think about exploring the wreck of the *Titanic* or any wreck in which people died?

Use of English: Revision of past tenses

Remember the differences between the tenses used to talk about the past.

Which verb tense is used in each sentence below? Use the descriptions in the box to help you.

a In April 1912, the ship set sail on its maiden voyage.
b It was making good progress across the Atlantic.
c A telegram was sent saying that the ship needed help.
d It took the *Carpathia* four hours to reach the place where the ship had sunk.
e "We have struck an iceberg."

Past simple: for something that happened at a particular time in the past and is completed

Present perfect: for something that started in the past and has a present result

Past continuous: for something that was happening around a particular time in the past

Past simple passive: when you don't know who did the action, or when it isn't important to know who did it

Past perfect simple: for something that happened before another event in the past

The Treasure Fleet

● What are big ships used for today?

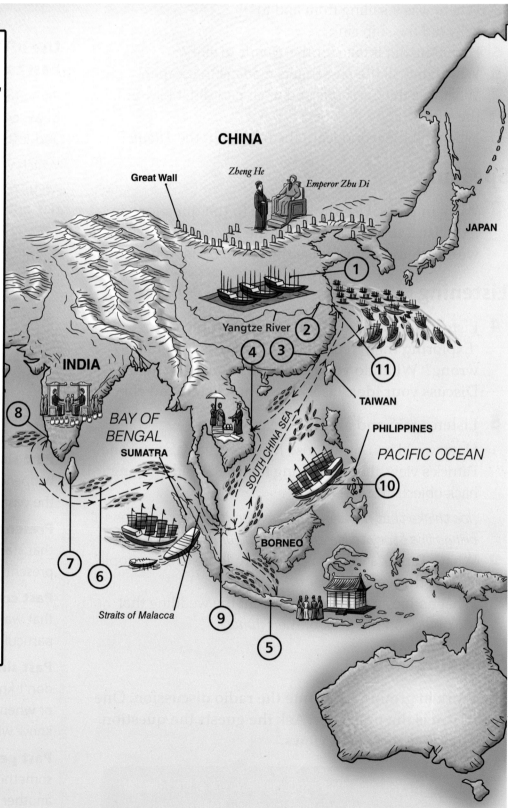

CHINA'S TREASURE FLEET
AMAZES THE WORLD
1405 - 07

1. Gigantic treasure ships are built in dry dock at **Longjiang**

2. Admiral Zheng He sets sail from **Nanjing**

3. The fleet waits at **Taiping** for favourable winds

4. Trading begins at **Champa (South Vietnam)** in Indo-China

5. Zheng He meets Chinese settlers on **Java**

6. Navigating by compass, the fleet crosses the **Indian Ocean**

7. Meets hostile reception from King of **Ceylon (Sri Lanka)**

8. Destination reached: bartering the ship's cargo for Indian goods at the port of **Calicut**

9. Zheng He clears pirates from the **Straits of Malacca**

10. The returning fleet is hit by a terrible storm

11. Triumphant reception on return to **Nanjing**

CHINA

Great Wall

Zheng He

Emperor Zhu Di

JAPAN

Yangtze River

INDIA

TAIWAN

PHILIPPINES

BAY OF BENGAL

SUMATRA

PACIFIC OCEAN

SOUTH CHINA SEA

Straits of Malacca

BORNEO

Listening

1 Before you listen, look at the map and read the information about China's Treasure Fleet.

2 Listen and follow the route on the map.

3 Listen to each section of the story again and answer the questions.

Section 1

1 Who was Zhu Di?
2 What kind of ship was a *junk*?
3 What was it like on board a *junk*?
4 Why did Zhu Di want a fleet of *junks*?

Section 2

5 What do we know about Zheng He's early life?
6 What did the emperor ask Zheng He to do and why?

Section 3

7 Which sea did they cross from Taiping to Champa?

Section 4

8 What did the Chinese fleet sell to the people in Champa?
9 What did the people of Champa give in return?

Section 5

10 To which island did Zheng He sail from Champa?
11 What was traded there?

Section 6

12 How did Zheng He's ships find their way across the ocean to Ceylon?

Section 7

13 Why didn't the Chinese fleet stay long in Ceylon?
14 What was the fleet's final destination?

Section 8

15 How long did the fleet stay in India?
16 What did they trade there?

Section 9

17 What happened in the Straits of Malacca?

Section 10

18 What happened as the fleet was sailing back across the South China Sea?
19 Why did the sailors think that St Elmo's Fire was a miracle?

Section 11

20 Was the emperor pleased with the expedition? How do you know?
21 What did the fleet bring back from the east coast of Africa?

Speaking

4 Work in groups. Retell the story of China's Treasure Fleet, using the information on the map and your answers to the questions in Exercise 3.

Should we continue to explore space?

● What do you know about space exploration?

1 Read the opinions. Which one is illustrated by the picture above? Which one do you agree with?

> I think we should find out more about the planets in our solar system. I don't think we'll ever live on another planet. It's interesting to know what they're like, though.

> I'm sure very large space stations will be built in the future. They'll be big enough for thousands of people to live on, which will be a good thing because soon there will be too many people for the earth. Space stations could help us to explore other planets, as well, to see if we could live there.

> What's the point of spending so much money on space exploration? It should be spent on solving problems on this planet.

Language tip

In spoken language:

● you can use *though* to mean *however*.

It's interesting to know what they're like, though.

● you can use *as well* to mean the same as *also* or *too*.

Space stations could help us to explore other planets, as well.

Both expressions usually go at the end of a clause or sentence.

Listening 9

2 Listen to this discussion about exploring space. Which of the following statements is correct?

1 All the students are in favour of space exploration.
2 The majority of the students are in favour.
3 A minority of the students are in favour.

3 Listen again and correct any incorrect information in these summaries of the students' opinions.

1 Aisha: We should keep on exploring space. One day people will live on the moon.
2 Oliver: We should send people to all the planets in our solar system, to find out more about them.
3 Cristina: Space tourism will be really popular in the future.
4 Tommy: Criminals will be sent to another planet or to a space station instead of prison.
5 Nicholas: People will need to live on other planets because the earth will get too hot, so we won't be able to live here.

Speaking

4 Work in groups. Discuss this question: Should we continue to explore space?

Writing

5 Complete these sentences to give your own predictions about space exploration.

1 People *will* / *won't* live ...
2 Animals *will* / *won't* be sent ...
3 Water *will* / *won't* be found ...
4 Life *will* / *won't* be discovered ...

Project: A great expedition

6 You're going to research and write about a great expedition, like Zheng He's on page 32. It can be a recent expedition or one from a long time ago.

1 First choose an explorer.   *Marco Polo*
2 Find out the following:
   ● When and where did they live?
   ● What do we know about their early life?
   ● Where did they travel from and to?
   ● Why did they go?
   ● What dangers did they meet?
   ● What did people think of them?
   ● How long were they away from home?
   ● What happened when they returned?
3 Use the questions above to organise your information under separate headings.
4 Write a first draft. Ask others to read it and comment on it.
5 Write a final draft. Find pictures to illustrate your project.
6 Give an illustrated presentation to the class about the explorer you have chosen.

> **Language tip**
>
> Use *will* to give information about the future or to predict what we think or guess will happen.
>
> ● *will* is often shortened to *'ll*
> *I don't think we'll ever live on another planet.*
>
> ● *will not* is often shortened to *won't*
> *There won't be enough room on earth.*
>
> ● The passive of the *will* future is *will* + *be* + past participle.
> *I'm sure very large space stations will be built in the future.*

Fiction

Chinua Achebe was a Nigerian author who wrote
novels, short stories, poetry and children's books.

1 Read the summary of the story so far. Who is the main character in
the story? What is his ambition?

The story so far

Chike and the River is a story about an eleven-year-old boy called Chike who
lives with his mother and two sisters in the village of Umuofia, in Nigeria. His
mother sends him to live with an uncle in Onitsha, a city on the River Niger.
Chike is so excited because he's always wanted to see the river ever since he
heard a story about it as a young child. But his mother tells him he must never
go near the river.

Chike lives with his uncle and his uncle's servant Michael and he goes to
school in Onitsha. He wants to cross the river on a ferry. He asks his uncle
for the money for the fare (a shilling), but he won't give it to him. Chike is
determined to find a way to get the money for the crossing.

2 Read Chapter 13 of the story and an extract from Chapter 14 on page 37.
Why is Chapter 13 called 'Chike's dream comes true'?

3 Read the extract again. Then answer the questions.
1 'Chike's chance came suddenly' *(line 1)* – his chance to do what?
2 What idea did Chike get from watching the three boys?
3 What did Chike learn from watching the boy who cleaned the enormously
long car?
4 How would you describe the way Chike approached the owner of the
small car?
5 How does Chike make sure he gets paid?
6 Why does Chike feel as proud as Mungo Park *(line 37)*?

4 Work in groups. Discuss these questions.
1 How does the author make Chike a sympathetic character?
2 Is there a particular story you remember from your childhood? What is it?
3 Is there something you've dreamed of doing since you were a child? What
is it?
4 Why do rivers fascinate people?

CHAPTER 13
Chike's dream comes true

Chike's chance came suddenly. It happened on a public holiday. His uncle had
gone to Umuofia for the holiday and was not expected back until the next day.
Chike ate his lunch quickly and went down to the riverside without saying a
word to Michael. Since he had no money, he did not think of crossing the river.

5   All he wanted to do was to watch the boats.
    When he got to the bank, he found many cars and lorries waiting to be
ferried. Then he saw three boys with buckets of water washing some of the cars.
He also saw that when they had finished the owners gave them some money.
"Why did I not think of this before?" he asked himself. He raced back home and

10 took a bucket of water and a piece of rag and ran all the way back. To his utter
disappointment, the boat had gone and there were no more cars around, only
lorries. But soon other cars began to arrive and Chike's hopes revived. So far
three had arrived. But they were all very small cars. Chike thought it would be
better to go for a big one with a wealthy owner. Soon an enormously long car

15 pulled up. Chike immediately approached it.
    The owner looked like a very important person. Perhaps he was a minister.
Then Chike lost his boldness. He stood by the car wondering what to say. But
while he hesitated one of the other boys marched up to the man and said, "Make
I wash your car, sir?"

20 At first the man ignored him but he did not give up. He spoke again, "Oga,
your car dorty plenty. I fit wash am fine."
    This time the man looked at him and nodded. The boy smiled and set to work.
Chike bit his lips. He said to himself, "If this boy can do it so can I."
    Then one small car arrived. Chike, no longer choosy, wasted no time at all. He

25 went up to the owner and in good English [said], "May I wash your car, sir? It is
very dirty and you are going to Lagos."
    The man smiled and said, "Go ahead."
    Chike filled his bucket with water from a nearby tap and set to work.
When he had finished he told the owner. But the man was busy talking to his

30 friend and paid little attention to Chike. He said, "Thank you" without looking at
Chike and continued talking. Chike stood there, shifting from one foot to the other.
Eventually the man looked at him again and put his hand into his pocket. Chike's
heart beat faster. He brought out a handful of coins and gave one to Chike.
    "Thank you, sir," said Chike. Then he looked at the coin and saw it was one

35 shilling. In his joy he said again, "Thank you, sir." The man did not reply; he was
talking to his friend again, with a cigarette in his mouth.

···

from CHAPTER 14

Chike on the boat

    During the journey Chike felt as proud as Mungo Park when he finally
reached the Niger. Here at last was the great River Niger. Chike stuck out his
chest as though he owned the river, and drew a deep breath. The air smelt clean

40 and fresh. He remembered another song at Umuofia and began to whistle it:
    Row, row, row your boat
    Gently down the stream
    Merrily, merrily, merrily, merrily,
    Life is but a dream.

---

ferried (line 7) taken by ferry

rag (line 10) a small piece of old cloth

utter (line 10) complete (used to emphasise something)

revived (line 12) brought back to life

pulled up (line 15) stopped (when talking about cars)

boldness (line 17) not being afraid of taking risks

hesitated (line 18) waited before doing something

marched up to (line 18) walked towards in a determined way

'Make I wash your car … ?' (line 18) = May I wash your car?

'Oga, your car dorty plenty. I fit wash am fine.' (line 21) = Sir, your car is very dirty. I can wash it very well.

choosy (line 24) choosing carefully, leaving out what is not so good

shifting (line 31) moving from one position to another

shilling (line 35) a coin used in the past

Mungo Park (line 37) Scottish explorer of Africa (1771–1806); he explored the River Niger.

Review of Units 3–4

Vocabulary

Rivers and coasts

1 Complete the sentences with the words from the box.

banks	coastline	floods
fresh water	rainfall	salt water

1 You usually find <u>fresh water</u> in rivers and lakes, whereas seas and oceans have ____.
2 People have lived along the ____ of the River Nile for thousands of years.
3 The east of Malaysia has a beautiful ____ with lots of lovely beaches.
4 One of the wettest places in South America is Lloró in Colombia where the annual ____ is about 13,000 millimetres.
5 ____ can cause problems for people who live near rivers.

2 Put these sentences in the correct places in the description of the water cycle at the top of the next column.

A This is called 'condensation'.
B The scientific word for this is 'precipitation'.
C They are blown inland by the wind.
D This is called 'run off'.
E This is called 'evaporation'.
F It is essential to life on Earth.

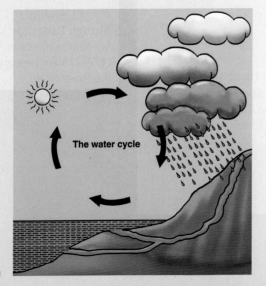

The water cycle

The water cycle

The water cycle is a continuous process. *It is essential to life on Earth.*[1]

The water in rivers, lakes and seas is heated by the sun and it turns into water vapour. The water vapour rises into the air. ____[2]

The water vapour is cooled as it rises and is changed back into tiny drops of liquid water. ____[3]

Clouds are formed. ____[4]

Clouds get heavy and water falls back to the earth as rain or snow. ____[5]

Rain water and melted snow are taken by rivers back to the sea. ____[6]

Use of English

3 Join these sentences using *which*.

1 The Caspian Sea is actually a lake. It is the largest enclosed body of water on Earth.
   The Caspian Sea, which is the largest enclosed body of water on Earth, is actually a lake.
2 The Atacama Desert is one of the driest places on Earth. It has an average rainfall of 15 millimetres per year.
3 The Red Sea has very salty water due to high evaporation. It is a sea inlet between Africa and Asia.
4 Lake Balaton is a fresh water lake in Hungary. It is the largest lake in central Europe.
5 The Panama Canal links the Atlantic Ocean with the Pacific Ocean. It is 77 kilometres long and was completed in 1914.

6 Norway has a coastline of 25,000 kilometres. This is surprising when you consider that it has a population of only five million people.

Norway has a coastline of 25,000 kilometres, which is surprising when you consider that it has a population of only five million people.

7 Ninety per cent of the wildlife in Madagascar is not found anywhere else in the world. This makes it a very interesting place for zoologists and other scientists.

8 The Aswan Dam has prevented flooding along the Nile. This has been good for people living in the area and for the economy of Egypt generally.

4 Use the phrases below to help you complete the sentences with *which / that* clauses.

- the best beaches are on the west side of the island
- there was a nature programme on TV last night
- we did a test yesterday
- you sent me some photos
- I needed a book for my project
- you thought the film was really good

1 Did you see the nature programme
which / that was on TV last night?
2 I couldn't find the book _____
_____.
3 The test _____
was very hard.
4 What was the title of the film _____
_____?
5 The photos _____
were really good.
6 The beaches _____
are the best.

General knowledge quiz

5 **Work with a partner. Ask and answer the questions.**
1 Which sea does the River Nile flow into?
2 Which are the biggest living reptiles in the world?
3 One of the sources of the Nile is Lake Tana in Ethiopia, the Blue Nile. What is the other source?
4 In ancient Egypt, what were flax and papyrus used for?
5 Is the Amazon River Basin north or south of the equator?

6 Where is Robinson Crusoe island?
7 Where was the *Titanic* sailing from and to?
8 What was the name of the ship that came to the rescue of the *Titanic*?
9 In 1405, Zheng He set off on a great expedition. Why did he go? Name some of the places he visited.
10 Name three of the world's oceans and say where they are.

Sports and hobbies

- **Topics** Sports and sports equipment; sporting ability; hobbies
- **Use of English** Compound nouns; abstract nouns; present perfect continuous

Sport for all

- Why do people do sport? Is international sport important?

Listening 🔟

1 Listen to the commentaries and look at the pictures on this page. Which sport is it?

1 horse riding

Vocabulary

2 Play this vocabulary game with a partner. Take it in turns to define and describe a sports player or an item of sports equipment in the pictures on these pages. Your partner has to guess the word.

A: *You need these when you're riding a horse. You hold them in your hands and they help you to control the horse.*

B: *Reins.*

A: *Yes, that's right. Your turn.*

3 Play Kim's Game with a partner. Look at the pictures on these pages for 30 seconds. Then close your books. Can you remember all the words associated with each sport? Make a list.

Horse riding
rider, reins, saddle

skiing — goggles, pole, skis

ice skating — skate

boxing — boxing gloves, ring

athletics UK, track and field US — javelin, running, high jump

ice hockey — puck

rollerblading — elbow pads, rollerblades/in-line skates

snowboarding — snowboard

horse riding UK, horseback riding US — reins, rider, saddle

skateboarding — knee pads, skateboard

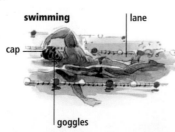

swimming — lane, cap, goggles

football UK, soccer US
- referee
- goal
- goalkeeper

American football UK, football US
- goal post
- helmet

basketball
- backboard
- basket

baseball
- cap
- pitcher
- glove/mitt
- batter

volleyball
- net

golf
- cup
- club
- caddie

rugby

cricket
- bowler
- stumps
- batsman

cycling
- helmet
- bicycle

tennis
- racket
- net

Listening 🔘11

4 Listen to the commentaries and identify the sports.

1 cricket

> ### Use of English: Compound nouns
>
> A compound noun is a noun with another noun, an adjective or a verb before it, e.g. *ice hockey*.

5 Answer the questions.

1 How many compound nouns can you find in the pictures?
2 Are there any which have an adjective as the first word?
3 How do you express these compound nouns in your language?

Speaking

6 Work in pairs. Ask and answer the questions in the quiz below.

> ### A question of sport
>
> 1 What does a football referee do?
>
> *He makes sure the players follow the rules.*
>
> 2 What does a goalkeeper do?
> 3 What does a golf caddie do?
> 4 In baseball, who throws the ball and who hits it?
> 5 In cricket, who throws the ball and who hits it?
> 6 In basketball, how do you score points?
> 7 Why is there a net on a tennis court?
> 8 Why are there stumps on a cricket pitch?

At the top of their game

What do you need to be a top athlete or sportsperson?

Reading

1 Who are the sportspeople mentioned in this article? Were they interested in sport from an early age?

Top qualities

Jessica Ennis-Hill was introduced to athletics at the age of ten, when her parents took her to a training event at a local stadium during the summer holidays. Her coach, whom she met at that first event, said that she was one of the most talented young athletes he had ever seen. She had strength, agility, co-ordination and speed but above all, determination. She's now an Olympic athlete who competes in the heptathlon.

Table tennis requires quick reactions, excellent hand-eye co-ordination and good powers of concentration. Together with competitiveness and steely determination, they have made Li Xiaoxia one of the best table tennis players in the world and have brought her success in the Olympics. "I'm very excited," Li said, when she won a gold medal. "This has been my dream since being a little girl. I dreamed of being an Olympic Champion." Li wasn't the favourite to win the event because her opponent, Ning Ding, had won the World Championship. After the final game, Li said "I was determined to win and I didn't back down".

Vocabulary

2 Find the abstract nouns in the article to complete this table.

Adjective	Noun
strong	
agile	
co-ordinated	
determined	
competitive	

Use of English: Abstract nouns

We usually use abstract nouns without *the* or *a / an*.

She had strength, agility, co-ordination and speed.

However, when you make an abstract noun specific rather than general, you use *the* or *a/an*.

She had the strength of someone twice her size.

3 Complete these sentences with the abstract nouns from Exercise 2.

1 <u>**Competitiveness**</u> is a quality of people for whom winning is very important.

2 If you can lift a very heavy weight, you have great _____.

3 If you play a racket sport, you need good hand–eye _____.

4 If you try very hard to do something difficult, you have great _____.

5 If you can move your whole body easily and quickly, you have great _____.

4 Here are four more abstract nouns from the text. Write sentences to show what they mean.

1 speed

2 concentration

3 success

Comprehension

5 Write questions for these answers.

1 Q: *How old was Jessica Ennis-Hill when she went to her first athletics event?*
A: She was ten.

2 Q: _____
A: He said that she was one of the most talented young athletes he had ever seen.

3 Q: _____
A: Quick reactions, excellent hand–eye co-ordination and good powers of concentration.

4 Q: _____
A: She's one of the best table tennis players in the world.

5 Q: _____
A: She had dreamed of being an Olympic champion.

Speaking

6 Work in groups. Discuss these questions.

1 What are the qualities you need to be a top athlete?
Strength, agility, ...

2 Which do you think is the most important of these?

3 Are some qualities needed for some sports more than others? Give examples.

4 Think of sportsmen and sportswomen you admire. What are the qualities or other factors that have made them successful?

What are your hobbies?

- What is a hobby? Why do people have hobbies?

Reading

1 Read what these 12- and 13-year-olds say about their hobbies. Do any of them have the same hobbies as you?

1 "My hobbies are playing the drums and trampolining."

2 "I LOVE karate!"

3 "I love reading, playing the guitar and singing. People say children watch TV and play video games all the time. However, only some kids do. Most kids like doing lots of activities."

4 "I love doing judo at my local club. I've been doing it for seven years and I'm now a black belt."

5 "I collect sweets – and then eat them! I also collect pencil cases. In total, I have about 50. I just love collecting them."

6 "I kick a stick down the street whenever I see one. It's not a hobby, but I just enjoy doing it. And I make model planes, as well."

7 "I collect coins. I have loads of foreign ones."

8 "I don't do any sports. I love juggling. I just can't stop doing it. I sometimes juggle in Maths, with pencil sharpeners!"

9 "I like to draw. I draw things I see on TV and in magazines. I collect leaves from trees, too. I like to make bookmarks from them."

10 "I love to write. I do it all the time. I keep talking to my friends and family about my stories, and they're starting to get a bit bored!"

11 "I collected shells when I was younger, but I threw them out a long time ago. Now I collect beads, jewellery and posters."

12 "My hobbies are acting and singing. I've been acting since I was two."

Vocabulary

2 Work with a partner. Make lists of the hobbies in Exercise 1 under the following headings:

- Sports / martial arts
- Collecting things
- Music and performing
- Art and other creative activities

3 Make true sentences about the children interviewed in Exercise 1 and their hobbies.

1 All of them
2 A third of them
3 A quarter of them
4 Two of them
5 One of them
6 None of them

a collect things.
b collects stamps.
c do sports/martial arts.
d enjoys art.
e have at least one hobby.
f make things.

4 Write a web forum post about your hobbies.

1 What are your hobbies?
2 How long have you been doing them?

Speaking

5 Work with a partner. Ask and answer these questions.

1 Does anyone in Exercise 1 say anything that you find funny?
2 Which of the hobbies mentioned in Exercise 1 do you find unusual?
3 Which of the hobbies in Exercise 1 did you do when you were younger?
4 Which of the hobbies in Exercise 1 would you like to do?

Use of English: Present perfect continuous

Use the present perfect continuous to talk about actions continuing up to now, especially with *for* and *since* to say how long they have lasted.

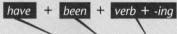

have + *been* + *verb + -ing*

I love judo. I've been doing it for seven years.

I've been acting since I was two.

Project: An after-school club

6 Your school wants some ideas for after-school clubs where students can try some new hobbies. With a partner, decide on an activity for an after-school club. Design and write a flyer for the activity.

- **Topics** Free time; the circus; a film review
- **Use of English** Phrasal verbs; position of adverbs

What are you into?

- In your free time, do you prefer staying in or going out?

Reading

1 Read what Lucía and Ramesh say. How are they similar? How are they different?

What are you into?

I've taken up the flute recently and I'm really into it. I've been playing the piano since I was six, but I'd never tried any other instrument. I went to see the Simón Bolívar youth orchestra when they came to Mexico City. It was wonderful. I knew then that I wanted to play in an orchestra and I loved the sound of the flute. What else do I do in my free time? Well, I enjoy playing volleyball and I go swimming. I sometimes go out with my friends to the cinema and they come round to my house. My mum says I do too much and that I should give something up, but I love doing lots of things.

Lucía, 13, Mexico City

I do taekwondo. It's a martial art. It's different from karate because there's more kicking. It helps you to develop strength, speed, balance and agility. It's really good. I love it! I don't do many other things. I prefer doing taekwondo to doing team sports, like football. I don't mind staying in, especially if I've just been to a taekwondo class. I just listen to some music on my iPod and chill out. I like watching TV and playing video games too. I usually go out with my family to a restaurant at the weekend.

Ramesh, 13, Kuala Lumpur

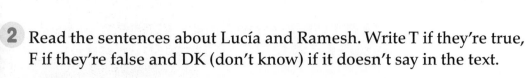

2 Read the sentences about Lucía and Ramesh. Write T if they're true, F if they're false and DK (don't know) if it doesn't say in the text.

Lucía

1 really enjoys playing the flute.   *True*
2 has been playing the flute for a long time.
3 went to an orchestral concert.
4 likes collecting musical instruments.
5 agrees with her mum about doing a lot of free-time activities.

Ramesh

6 has been doing taekwondo for a long time.
7 thinks doing taekwondo is good for general fitness.
8 does a lot of different sports and activities in his free time.
9 likes to relax after a taekwondo class.
10 prefers eating in a restaurant to eating at home.

3 Find examples in the blogs of verbs followed by the *-ing* form.

I enjoy playing volleyball.

Speaking

4 Work with a partner.

1 Which of the things Lucía and Ramesh say are exactly the same for you?
2 Can you adapt any of the things they say to make them true for you?

Listening 12

5 Listen. Who's talking?

6 Listen again. Who's talking to a friend? Who's giving a talk at school? Give reasons for your answer.

7 Listen again and write down what the first person says. Underline the words and phrases which you'd use in conversation but not in a formal talk.

8 Work with a partner. Find the following phrasal verbs in the text. Explain what each one means.

1 take up

start doing something, for example, a new hobby. So, Lucía has just started playing the flute.

Language tip

Verb followed by the *-ing* form

Use an *-ing* form after these verbs:

enjoy   don't mind

You can also use an *-ing* form after these verbs:

like   love   prefer

---

2 be into
3 go out
4 come round
5 give up
6 stay in
7 chill out

Writing

9 Write a short paragraph about your free-time activities. Use the texts in Exercise 1 as a model.

Use of English: Phrasal verbs

Phrasal verbs are made up of two or more words, e.g. *take up, go out.*

They're used a lot in English. Try to learn a few at a time and try to learn them in the context of a particular topic.

At the circus

- Look at the photos of two kinds of circus on these pages. What do you think the difference is?

Reading

1 Read this article about Duffy's Circus. Do the circus performers enjoy their work?

Vocabulary

2 Find the words in the article for the following:

1 someone who entertains people by …
  - **a** doing difficult physical acts   *acrobat*
  - **b** keeping several balls or other objects in the air
  - **c** doing silly things to make people laugh
2 a group of circus performers
3 the place where a circus performance takes place

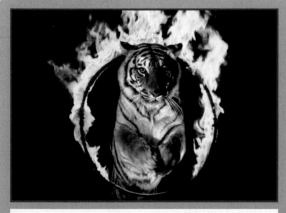

A tiger jumps through a hoop and lands on a stool. There is a safety net between the animals and the audience. What do you think about using animals in circuses?

The Circus – a way of life

Duffy's Circus has been entertaining audiences for over 200 years.

The performers are an international mix of Moroccans, Hungarians, Ukrainians, Latvians, Russians, Chinese, Australians, Irish, English, Moldovans, Mongolians and Mexicans. Some work with the animals, such as tigers and horses; others are acrobats, jugglers and clowns.

During the nine-month season, in which they visit 80 towns, the troupe lives on site in caravans, working and socialising together.

"It is hard work," says Liana, an acrobat from Ukraine, "but you get used to it."

It's 8.30 in the morning and Liana is already practising for the afternoon performance, which starts at 2 o'clock.

Liana was only two years old when she entered the circus ring. She and her friend David, who's from Mexico, both come from performing families. So they only know life in the circus. "Life is always interesting. We're always travelling around, meeting new people and learning a lot," says Liana.

She always goes home to Ukraine at the end of the season in October for two or three months. However, she finds it hard to stay in one place for long. She can't wait to get back to the circus. "I'll definitely stay with the circus as long as I can, because I can never imagine myself doing any other kind of job."

David is putting on his clown make-up. He is a fifth-generation circus entertainer. He has been performing in the circus ring since he was just 16 months old. "I have family all over the world in the circus," he says. "This is normal life for me."

Tom, who is a teenage member of the Duffy family, specialises in doing back flips and juggling on the back of a horse. "We normally practise from about 8 am to 11 am. There isn't much time off during the day, so after the shows at night we just have a couple of hours to chill out before we go to bed. I really enjoy that."

Comprehension

3 Answer the questions.

1 Who are the performers in Duffy's circus?   *Animals, acrobats, ...*
2 How does Liana feel about being in the circus?
3 What do Liana, David and Tom have in common?
4 Do you think they will all go on working in the circus? Give your reasons.

4 Rewrite these sentences putting the adverbs in the correct place.

1 We go to the cinema at the weekend. *(often)*
   We often go to the cinema at the weekend.
2 I'll stay with the circus all my life. *(definitely)*
3 You need good hand–eye co-ordination to be a juggler. *(certainly)*
4 I can get you a ticket for the circus. *(probably)*
5 At the end of the evening, I relax in my caravan. *(just)*
6 The tigers will jump through hoops for their trainer. *(only)*

Listening 13

5 The picture shows the Cirque du Soleil. Do you think it's similar to Duffy's Circus? Listen and find out more.

6 Listen again and answer these questions.

1 Where is the Cirque du Soleil from?
2 Where does it perform?
3 What do we know about the performers?
4 How is the Cirque du Soleil different from most circuses?
5 What is the Cirque du Soleil's view on animals in circuses?

Speaking

7 Work in groups. Discuss these questions.

1 Would you like to go to see one of these circuses? Why?
2 Why do you think Liana, David and Tom like working in the circus?
3 How would you feel about spending a week working at one of these circuses? Which one would you choose?
4 Should animals be used in circuses?

> **Use of English: Position of adverbs**
>
> These adverbs go **before** main verbs, but **after** the verb *be* and auxiliary verbs / modals, e.g. *have, will, can, must, should,* etc.:
>
> * adverbs of frequency: *always, often, usually / normally, sometimes, never*
> * adverbs of certainty: *certainly, definitely, probably*
> * other adverbs: *already, also, only, just, still, even*
>
> Find examples of the adverbs above in the article about Duffy's Circus. Notice that *all, both* and *each* follow the same rules.
> *She and her friend David both come from performing families.*

A film review

- What would you expect to read in a film review? Why do people write them? Why do people read them?

Reading

1 Read this review of *Man of Steel*. What did the reviewer think of the film?

1 *Man of Steel* is the latest film about the superhero, Superman. It is directed by Zach Snyder and stars Henry Cavill as Clark Kent and Amy Adams as Lois Lane.

2 The film is set in Kansas, USA. Clark Kent, the main character, is a reporter who works on a newspaper called *The Daily Planet*. His friend, Lois Lane, is also a journalist there. Clark Kent discovered, as a young boy, that he was different from other children because he had superhuman strength, speed and agility – and the ability to fly.

3 At the beginning of *Man of Steel*, we see Clark Kent as a baby, born on a distant planet called Krypton. He is sent to Earth, where he is adopted by the Kent family, who live on a farm in Smallville, Kansas. The film then moves forward in time. Nobody knows that Clark, a shy reporter, is actually Superman, the superhero who is able to save the world from disasters. However, the evil criminal General Zod arrives on the scene. When Zod discovers that Clark Kent is Superman, he attacks his parents' farm. Superman defends his home and defeats Zod.

4 Henry Cavill plays the part of Superman. While he is particularly good as the shy, modest Clark Kent, he's also convincing as the superhero, Superman. Amy Adams gives a good performance as Lois, warm and funny as well as clever and tough.

5 The script is well written and the special effects, particularly in the final battle scene, are impressive. The soundtrack for the film is dramatic and inspiring. Overall, the film is definitely worth seeing.

2 Read the film review again. Choose a heading for each paragraph.

Summary of the plot ①
Introduction to the film ②
Opinion of the film ③
The actors and the acting ④
Setting and main characters ⑤

Speaking

3 Work with a partner. Ask and answer the questions about *Man of Steel*.

1 Who is the film directed by?
2 Where is it set?
3 What happens at the beginning?
4 Who plays the part of Clark Kent / Superman?

(For the following three questions, you can give your own opinions if you've seen the film.)

5 What can you say about the performances of the main actors?
6 What can you say about the script, the special effects and the soundtrack?
7 Would you recommend this film?

4 Work with a partner. Make a list of the positive things you can say about a film.

The script was well written. ...

Now make a list of the negative things you can say.

(The main actor) wasn't convincing.

5 Work in groups. Use the questions in Exercise 3, and your lists from Exercise 4, to talk about films you've seen.

A *I saw ... last week.*
B *Who was in it?*
C *What was it about?*
D *What did you think of it?*

Project: Write a film review

6 Write a film review for a classroom display called 'Films we like'. Work individually or in pairs.

1 Choose a film which you really like.
2 Use the headings in Exercise 2 to plan your review.
3 Make notes about what you will include under each heading.
4 Write the review using your notes and follow the style of the review of *Man of Steel*:

- use the present tense for the plot summary
- use some of the sentence adverbs, such as *however, at the beginning, while*
- use some of the expressions from the review, such as *he / she is particularly good as ... , he / she gives a good performance as ...*

5 Ask others to comment on your review.
6 Write a final version. Include a picture if you can.

Fiction

1 What do you know about David Beckham?

2 Read the summary of the story so far and the extract from Chapter 2 on page 53. Who is the narrator ('I') in the story?

> **The story so far**
>
> *Bend it like Beckham,* by Narinder Dhami, is the story of Jess, an Indian girl who loves football. Another girl, Jules, sees Jess playing football in the park with her friend Taz and some other boys. Jules takes Jess to a training session with her team, Hounslow Harriers. But first, Jess has to meet Joe, the team's coach.

3 Find these football words in the text.

1 the place where you play football
2 moved the ball forward with short kicks
3 the players who try to stop you reaching the goal
4 the line along each of the two longer sides of a sports field
5 the area in front of the goal
6 kicked with the side of the foot
7 it's attached to the goal posts to stop the ball
8 another word for 'team'
9 got a goal

4 Find these expressions in the text. What do they mean?

1 (I was) grinning from ear to ear. *(lines 4–5)*
2 I beamed. *(line 9)*
3 He frowned. *(line 10)*
4 My face fell. *(line 16)*
5 I glowed with pride. *(line 37)*

5 Read the text again and answer these questions.

1 How does Jess feel before she goes on to the pitch?
2 How does she feel when she's on the pitch?
3 How does she feel when she comes off the pitch?
4 How does Joe's attitude to Jess change and why?

6 Work in groups. Discuss these questions.

1 Can girls be as good as boys at football? What about other sports?
2 Are all sports suitable for both boys and girls?

Bend it Like Beckham

I took a deep breath, and ran out on to the pitch. Jules
had stopped to chat to Joe as I rushed over to them. The
first thing I noticed was that Joe didn't look too pleased
to see me. But that couldn't stop me grinning from ear to
5 ear. I was excited just to be there.

"Where do you usually play?" Joe said. No hello,
nothing. It would have sounded really off, if he hadn't
had such a soft Irish accent.

I beamed at him. "In the park."

10 He looked at Jules and frowned. "I meant, what
position?"

"Oh, sorry." I felt a bit of a fool. "I usually play all
over, but up front on the right is best."

Joe looked me up and down. "Get your boots on,
15 then," he said.

My face fell. "I haven't got any."

For a minute, I thought he was going to chuck me
out before I'd even got started. I stared at him anxiously,
trying to make him realise how desperate I was to play.
20 Jules was looking a bit uncomfortable. I guessed that
she'd had to persuade Joe to give me a go.

"All right," he said at last. "Join in and start warming up."

I smiled with relief, and unzipped my tracksuit top. I had my Beckham
shirt on underneath. Maybe soon I'd be wearing the Harriers strip like the
25 other girls. But first I had to show what I could do ...

I felt nervous as I took my place on the pitch with the other players. I
never felt nervous when I was playing against Taz and that lot, but this was
different. I had to do well to earn a place in the side.

But once the ball was at my feet, I lost all my nerves. It was just like
30 being back in the park. Adrenaline pumped through me as I dribbled down
the pitch, managing to avoid two defenders. I did my famous double-step
over the ball to get round a third and ran forward. I had the goal in my
sights.

"Pass to Jules!" I heard Joe yelling from the touchline.

35 I slid the ball across the box, straight into Jules' path, and she sidefooted
it into the net.

"Brilliant!" Joe called, and I glowed with pride. I wanted this so much
it *hurt*.

When the game was over, I was so nervous, I felt sick. I wanted to know
40 if I'd made it into the side. I *thought* I'd done well – I hadn't scored myself
but I'd set up goals for Jules and another girl whose name I didn't know. As
we trooped off the pitch, I felt my heart lurch as Joe came over to me and
took me to one side.

"How'd it feel out there?" he asked.

45 "Excellent," I gasped. I was red in the face and out of breath but I felt
fantastic. "Really great."

Joe looked at me curiously. "I've never seen an Indian girl into football."

I smiled shyly at him. "I would have come sooner, but I didn't even
know they had a girls' team here."

by Narinder Dhami

rushed *(line 2)* hurried

**(it would have sounded)
really off** *(line 7)* very
unfriendly

I felt a bit of a fool *(line 12)*
I felt silly

**(I thought he was going to)
chuck me out** *(lines 17–18)*
make me leave

to give me a go *(line 21)* give
me a chance

the Harriers strip *(line 24)* the
shirt and shorts worn by the
Harriers team

that lot *(line 27)* those people

yelling *(line 34)* shouting
loudly

if I'd made it into the side
(line 40) if I'd been successful in
getting into the team

I'd set up goals *(line 41)* I'd
made it possible for someone
to score goals

trooped off *(line 42)* walked off
together in a group

lurch *(line 42)* suddenly move
in a way that is not controlled

gasped *(line 45)* breathed
quickly and deeply

Review of Units 5–6

Vocabulary

Sports and sports equipment

1 Choose the odd one out and give your reason in each case.

1. **a** footballer   **b** referee
   c goalkeeper   **d** bowler
2. **a** boxing   **b** cricket
   c rugby   **d** football
3. **a** bat   **b** racket
   c pole   **d** club
4. **a** caddie   **b** batsman
   c rider   **d** snowboard
5. **a** elbow pads   **b** knee pads
   c helmet   **d** reins
6. **a** volleyball   **b** rugby
   c puck   **d** basketball

1 *b Referee is the odd one out because the others are all sports players.*

OR

d Bowler is the odd one out because a bowler is connected with cricket, whereas all the others are connected with football.

Hobbies

2 Put the words from the box in the correct column. Some can go in more than one column.

beads	bookmarks	coins
drums	guitar	judo
karate	model planes	posters
shells		

Play	Collect	Do	Make

Use of English

3 Complete the second sentence by changing the adjective from the first sentence to an abstract noun.

1. She's a very successful athlete.
   She enjoyed *success* at an early age.
2. You need to be strong to be good at most sports.
   _____ is important for most sports.
3. Acrobats have to be very agile.
   One of the most important qualities for an acrobat is _____.
4. To be a good tennis or badminton player, your movements need to be well co-ordinated. Good _____ is particularly important for sports like tennis and badminton.
5. For some people, taking part in a sport is more important than being competitive. For some people, participation is more important than _____.
6. Are you determined to succeed?
   Do you have enough _____ to be successful?

4 Complete the sentences with the words from the box.

| up | in | round | into | out |

1. I gave __up__ playing the guitar because I didn't have time to practise.
2. You're very good at juggling. When did you take it _____?
3. My cousin is _____ martial arts. She does judo, taekwondo and karate.
4. Do you want to go _____ at the weekend?
5. Come _____ at 6 o'clock and we'll do our homework together before the film starts.
6. I like spending time with my friends, but sometimes I enjoy just staying _____ and chilling _____.

5 Write a caption for each picture using the present perfect continuous.

1 *She's been painting.*

2

3

4

5 since 8 o'clock this morning.

6 since she was five years old.

6 Re-order the words to make sentences.

1 definitely / I'd / to / see / like / the Cirque du Soleil
I'd definitely like to see the Cirque du Soleil.

2 the / play / We / tennis / in / often / park

3 been / We've / just / swimming / lake / in / the

4 well / do / He'll / in / long jump / certainly / the

5 play / friends / I / volleyball / the / on / beach / My / and / sometimes

6 tall / usually / Basketball / are / players / very

7 already / I've / seen / the / film / twice / *Superman*

8 grandmother's / she / My / in / goes / seventies / her / and / still / skiing

General knowledge quiz

7 **Work with a partner. Ask and answer the questions.**

1 What do you call the person who throws the ball in baseball?

2 What do you call the person who hits the ball in cricket?

3 Name three events in athletics.

4 How many sports are there in a triathlon, heptathlon and decathlon?

5 Name three martial arts.

6 What is special about the Simón Bolívar Orchestra?

7 Where is the Cirque du Soleil from?

8 What is special about the Cirque du Soleil?

9 Who is Clark Kent?

10 What is Clark Kent's job?

7 Household routines

- **Topics** Kitchen appliances and equipment; talking about your room; jobs at home
- **Use of English** Phrasal verbs (kitchen and home); compound nouns; compound adjectives for colours; comparative adjectives with *much, far ... than, a lot less ... than, just as ... as, nowhere near as ... as*

In the kitchen

- Look at the picture. Which things did people not have 100 years ago?

Vocabulary

1 Look at the picture. Match the words to the kitchen appliances and equipment.

a bin	**e** fridge	**i** microwave	**m** teapot
b blender	**f** hob	**j** oven	**n** toaster
c dishwasher	**g** iron	**k** saucepan	
d freezer	**h** wok	**l** scales	

2 Use the words below to make compound nouns for kitchen appliances and equipment.

1	coffee	6	remote	a	fan
2	washing	7	fire	b	extinguisher
3	extractor	8	food	c	processor
4	tin	9	ironing	d	pan
5	frying	10	light	e	control

f	opener
g	board
h	switch
i	machine
j	machine

3 Work with a partner. Ask and answer about the items in Exercise 2.

A *What number is the coffee machine?*

B *It's number ...*

Listening 14

4 Listen to these conversations. Link each one to an item in the picture.

5 Listen again. Which conversations take place in a formal situation (where the people don't know each other very well)?

6 Complete these extracts from the conversations in Exercise 4 with the correct phrasal verbs. Then listen again and check.

1 It's really dark in here. Can I __*put*__ the light __*on*__?

2 Would you mind if I _____ this _____ in the microwave?

3 Would you mind emptying the dishwasher and _____ the things _____?

4 _____ the extractor fan _____. I can't hear myself speak!

5 Would you mind if I _____ the TV _____? It's really useful for me to listen to the news.

6 **A** _____ the scales _____. I'm going to make a cake.

B Remember to _____ afterwards.

7 Work with a partner. Take turns to be an exchange student and a host. Make up conversations using *Would you mind ...?* and the items in the picture in Exercise 1. You can also use some of the phrasal verbs in Exercise 6.

Exchange student: *Would you mind if I put the TV on?*

Host: *Not at all. Go ahead.*

Language tip

To ask if you can do something, use *Would you mind if I* + verb in the past tense.

Would you mind if I switched the TV off?

To ask someone else to do something, use *Would you mind* followed by verb + *-ing*.

Would you mind switching the TV off?

Use of English: Phrasal verbs

Phrasal verbs are verbs made up of two or more words, e.g. *turn down, switch off*. They are very common in English. Try to learn them in context. Here the context is the kitchen and life at home.

In my room

- How much time do you spend in your room at home?

Inside teenagers' rooms

Zara's room

Zara's room is at the top of the house. It's pale blue. There isn't much on the walls, apart from a noticeboard where she puts photos, pictures and the certificates she got for her piano exams. Her mother isn't keen on her putting up pictures on the walls. If Zara had her way, the room would have pictures on all the walls. It would be painted lime green, with one wall papered in a different colour, and it would have a balcony. But for now, to add colour and interest, she has a pink and white bedspread, some purple cushions in the shape of hearts and some bright pink cushions in the shape of flowers, and lights around the bed. There's an alarm clock and a lamp next to her bed and she's got four storage baskets under the bed, for shoes and for the soft toys she has kept from childhood. There's a wardrobe for her clothes and there are bookshelves next to the wardrobe. "I've got quite a lot in my room," she says, "and it sometimes gets messy, but I don't care. I always know where everything is!"

Reading

1 Read about Zara's room and Jake's room. What do you like about them? Is there anything you don't like?

2 Work in pairs. Ask and answer these questions about Zara and Jake.

1 What do their rooms tell you about them?
2 Is there anything Zara and Jake have in common?
3 What do they mention that you can see in the pictures?
4 What do they mention that you can't see in the pictures?
5 What can you see in the pictures that they don't mention?
6 *If Zara had her way, the room would have pictures on all the walls.* What does this mean?
7 Who do you think is most satisfied with their room?
8 Does a room always tell you something about the person who lives there?

3 In pairs, you are going to try to remember what is in Zara's room, giving details of colour and position. Look at the picture of the room for 10 seconds. Then close your books.

Jake lives in a flat. His room is quite plain, with cream walls and a pale grey carpet. However, he's got a lot of pictures on the walls, so they add interest to the room. He keeps his room tidy. His clothes are hung neatly in the cupboard next to the bunk beds. He sleeps on the top bunk; the bottom bunk turns into a sofa, which is great for chilling out. Some of his books are in the bookcase; the rest are carefully stacked in piles in one corner of the room. He's taken up the guitar recently and he's really into it. He's been writing songs, which he enjoys playing to friends. He's also keen on football. Next to the bunk beds, there's a small table which holds the football trophies and medals he has won. Above the table are two shelves where he keeps his collection of toy cars. "I'd always keep those," he says. "I was crazy about cars from a very early age. I knew every car on the road!"

Jake's room

Speaking

4 Interview your partner about their room. Make notes of their answers.

1 Is your room neat and tidy, or messy?
2 What colour is it?
3 What have you got on the walls?
4 What else is there in your room?
5 Is your room how you like it? What would you change?

Ask your partner to check that the notes you've written are correct.

Language tip

To give a precise description of a colour, you can use compound adjectives:

adjective + adjective

It's pale blue.
some bright pink cushions

noun + adjective

It would be painted lime green.

Writing

5 Write a description of your partner's room. Use the descriptions in Exercise 1 as a model. Include some quotes from your partner – remember to use speech marks ("...").

Jobs at home

- What are the jobs that you do regularly at home?

Listening and reading 15

1 Listen to Lee and Tina doing this quiz. Who is tidier? Who is more helpful around the house? Who is more practical? Tina asks the questions. . .

Part 1 How tidy are you?

1 How often do you tidy your room? (Once a week? Twice a week? Once a month?)
2 How would you describe your room?
   a It's always neat and tidy.
   b It's quite tidy.
   c When it gets really messy and I can't find anything, I tidy it up.
   d It's always a complete mess.

3 How often do you make your own bed? (Always? Sometimes? At the weekend? Never?)

Part 2 How helpful are you?

4 Do you ever put the rubbish out?
   a Yes, I do it every day.
   b I do it when I'm asked to do it.
   c I don't like putting the rubbish out, so I try to have a good excuse ready.
   d No, never. It's a horrible job.

5 Who sets the table? Who clears the table? Do you ever help?
6 Who does the washing up? Do you ever help?
7 Do you ever clean the bathroom?
   a Yes, quite often.
   b Sometimes.
   c Only when I'm paid to do it.
   d You must be joking!

Part 3 How practical are you?

8 Could you prepare dinner? What would you make?
9 Do you know how to iron a shirt? Which part of the shirt do you start with?
10 What would you do if a button had come off your school shirt?
   a I'd sew it on.
   b I'd ask someone to show me how to sew it on.
   c I'd ask someone else to sew it on.
   d I'd throw it away.

2 Work with a partner. Ask and answer the questions in the quiz.
Give your partner a mark out of three for each question:

3 = you're very helpful at home

2 = you're quite helpful at home

1 = you're OK, but you could do more

0 = lazybones!

Use of English: Comparisons

To make comparisons stronger, you can use phrases such as:

much	much tidier than, much more practical than
far ... than	far tidier than, far more practical than
a lot less ... than	a lot less tidy than, a lot less practical than
nowhere near as ... as	nowhere near as tidy as, nowhere near as practical as

You're far tidier than me.

I'm a lot less helpful than you.

I'm nowhere near as practical as you.

To make comparisons stronger between things that are equal, use *just as ... as*.

You're just as untidy as me!

3 Use the following phrases and adjectives to compare Zara's room with Jake's room (pages 58 and 59).

far ... than	colourful
a lot less ... than	plain
nowhere near as ... as	tidy
just as ... as	interesting

Zara's room is ... than / as Jake's room.

4 Use your answers to the quiz in Exercise 1 to make comparisons between yourself and your partner.

> You're far tidier than I am.

> Maybe. But I'm nowhere near as practical as you are.

Project: Design your own room

5 Design your ideal room.

1 Draw and label a plan.
2 Include the following details in your plan: furniture, colours, lights, appliances, decoration.
3 Find pictures to illustrate what you would like.
4 Write a description of your room to feature in a magazine.

- **Topics** Tropical rainforests; photosynthesis and aerobic respiration; farming in Kenya; food chains and the effect of habitat changes
- **Use of English** Present passive; present perfect active and passive

Rainforests

- Why are rainforests important?

Listening 16

1 Listen. What sort of TV programme is this?

2 Listen and complete the fact file.

Tropical Rainforests

1 Tropical rainforests cover _____% of the world's land surface.
2 The largest rainforest is the _____.
3 Rainforests are home to _____ of the earth's wildlife and _____ of its plants.
4 _____% of our modern medicines come from the rainforests.
5 Food from the rainforest includes: nuts, bananas, spices, coffee and _____.
6 The Amazon rainforest holds more than _____ of the earth's rainwater.
7 The trees in the rainforests keep the air clean by taking in _____ and producing the _____ we need to breathe.

3 Listen again and answer the questions.

1 How many countries in South America have rainforest areas?
2 Why are plants important for the animals who live in the rainforest?
3 Where does the anti-malaria drug quinine come from?
4 Why is the rainforest important for medical research?
5 Why do we often see mist and clouds above the rainforest?

Speaking

4 Work with a partner. Discuss these questions.

1 Why are rainforests called 'the lungs of the earth'?
2 Why do we need parks and gardens in a city?

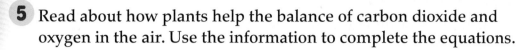

Reading

5 Read about how plants help the balance of carbon dioxide and oxygen in the air. Use the information to complete the equations.

Photosynthesis

Plants take in carbon dioxide from the air through their leaves. They take up water from the ground through their roots. Combined with the energy from sunlight, this makes the plants release oxygen into the air and produces glucose in the plant: the oxygen is released into the air through the leaves; the glucose is needed by the plant for energy. This process is called photosynthesis:

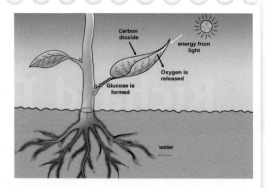

carbon dioxide + _____ (+ light energy) ⟶ glucose + oxygen

Aerobic respiration

All plants and animals need energy to stay alive. Plants get their energy from a combination of glucose and oxygen. Glucose and oxygen are changed into carbon dioxide and water, in a process called aerobic respiration:

glucose + _____ ⟶ carbon dioxide + water (+ energy)

6 Why are the following important for plants?
1 leaves
2 roots
3 sunlight
4 glucose

Listening 17

7 Listen to Amber and Zahra doing their Science homework. Help them to complete the worksheet their teacher has given them.

Use of English: The present passive

In scientific and technical writing, the passive is often used. This is because we focus on the action, not the person or the thing that does the action.

| be present tense | past participle |

Oxygen is released into the air through the leaves.

Glucose and oxygen are changed into carbon dioxide and water.

Photosynthesis and aerobic respiration

When there is bright light ...
There is more photosynthesis than respiration.
So carbon dioxide *is taken in*[1] and oxygen _____[2]. More oxygen than carbon dioxide _____[3].

When there is dim light ...
There is equal photosynthesis and respiration.
No gases _____[4]. In other words, oxygen and carbon dioxide _____[5] or _____[6].

When it's dark ...
There is respiration, but there is no photosynthesis. Oxygen _____[7] and carbon dioxide _____[8].
More carbon dioxide than oxygen _____[9].

Live and let live

- What sort of problems do you think farmers in Africa have?

Reading

1 Read the article. What problem did Richard's parents have on their farm?

Richard Turere: inventor

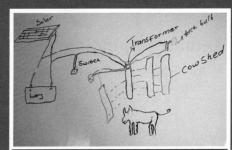

This is Richard's diagram showing how the lion lights work.

Richard Turere has always enjoyed making things using old household appliances and machines. For example, when he was quite young, he made fans for his parents' house from car parts and things he found in a junkyard.

Richard lives on the edge of the Nairobi National Park in Kenya. The park is full of rhino, giraffe, buffalo and lions.

Since he was nine, Richard has had the job of looking after his family's cows, goats and sheep. The big problem has been the lions. "I grew up hating lions," says Richard. "They used to come at night and feed on our cattle when we were sleeping."

Then one night, as he was walking around with a torch, he noticed something. "I discovered that the lions were scared of the moving light." Lions are naturally afraid of people. Richard realised that the lions linked the moving torchlight with people, so they stayed away. Using some bulbs and wires, Richard set up a series of flashing lights to give the impression that people were walking around the land where the animals were kept. The lions didn't come near. Soon other families were using his 'lion lights'.

Richard's lion lights cost just ten dollars to make. They have not only helped the farmers but also the lions. Many lions have been killed by farmers trying to protect their animals. Now, across Kenya, Richard's idea has been adopted by farmers to protect their animals from predators and to protect their crops from elephants.

Richard has been offered a scholarship at one of Kenya's top schools. "One year ago, I was just a boy herding my father's cows. Now I want to be an engineer and a pilot."

Sources: www.edition.cnn.com and www.nationalgeographic.com

2 Look at the caption for Richard's drawing. Write similar captions for the two photos.

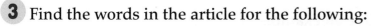

Vocabulary

3 Find the words in the article for the following:

1 pieces of electrical equipment, like washing machines and ovens, used in people's houses
2 a place where old, unwanted things can be left, bought and sold
3 the side, the part that is furthest from the centre
4 a small electric light that you carry in your hand
5 animals that kill and eat other animals
6 plants grown by farmers for food
7 keeping animals together in a group
8 someone who designs or builds things such as roads, railways, bridges or machines
9 someone who flies a plane.

4 Answer the questions.

1 How does Richard's early life relate to his ambitions now?
2 Why is Richard's invention good for man and nature?
3 Why is Richard's invention such a good idea?
4 How has Richard's invention changed his life?

5 Complete the sentences using the verbs in brackets. Remember to use the present perfect passive.

1 All Richard's inventions *have been made* from simple things and old appliances. (*make*)
2 Richard _____ to speak about his invention at a conference in California. (*invite*)
3 He _____ a place at a top high school in Kenya. (*give*)
4 The lion lights _____ by environmentalists because they are powered by solar energy and they protect wildlife. (*welcome*)
5 The lives of both the farm animals and the lions _____, thanks to Richard's invention. (*save*)
6 Crops _____ from elephants by Richard's lion lights. (*protect*)

Speaking

6 Work in small groups. Discuss these questions.

1 What are the advantages of Richard's invention?
2 Are there any disadvantages?

Writing

7 You've just heard about Richard's invention. Write a tweet (maximum 140 letters and spaces) describing it to a friend.

Use of English: The present perfect active and passive

Use the present perfect for situations continuing up to now and for things that have happened, but are not linked to a specific past time.

Active

| *have* present tense | past participle |

The big problem *has been* the lions.

Richard Turere *has* always *enjoyed* making things using old household appliances and machines.

Passive

| *have / has been* | past participle |

Richard's idea *has been adopted* by farmers to protect their animals from predators.

Many lions *have been killed* by farmers trying to protect their animals.

The food chain

What does a food chain describe? Can you give an example of a food chain?

This pyramid shows part of the food chain in Kenya. Grass is eaten by cows, sheep, goats, zebras and similar animals. Leaves are eaten by giraffes. All these animals are eaten by lions.

Reading

1 Read these definitions. Then use the words to describe the animals and plants in the pyramid.

Grass is a producer. It is eaten by ...

predator an animal that kills and eats other animals

prey an animal that is hunted and eaten by another animal

herbivore an animal that only eats plants

carnivore an animal that eats other animals

producer (in a food chain) a plant that makes its own food by photosynthesis

consumer (in a food chain) an animal that eats a plant or another animal

Did you know?

An apex predator is a predator at the top of a food chain. It has no natural predators. A lion is an apex predator. (The word *apex* means 'the highest part of a shape', so we can talk of 'the apex of a pyramid' or 'the apex of a triangle'.)

Can you think of any other apex predators? Where do they live?

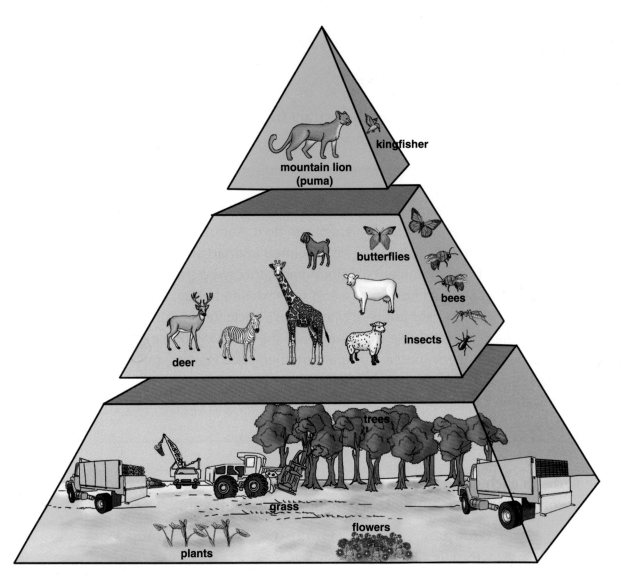

Listening 🔘18

2 Listen to *Junior Science Watch*. As you listen, find the animals in the picture.

3 Write down what you can remember from the radio programme about what can go wrong with the food chain. Use the diagram to help you.

4 Work in small groups. Compare the notes you wrote for Exercise 3. Put them together to complete a summary of how human activity can affect the food chain.

5 Read out your summaries to the class and compare them.

Project: Animals and the food chain

6 Give a presentation about three animals.

1 Choose three animals: a mammal, a bird and a reptile or an amphibian.
2 For each one, find out:
   ● whether it's a carnivore, a herbivore or an omnivore (eats plants and animals)
   ● what it eats
   ● why it's important in the food chain.
3 Draw a diagram for each one, showing its place in the food chain.
4 Give a presentation of your chosen animals to the class.

Fiction

1 What do you know about the Maori people?

2 Read the summary of the story so far and the extract from Chapter 13. What does Kahu do and why?

The story so far

Maoris believe that leadership is hereditary: it passes to the first-born son and then to his first son. In *The Whale Rider* by Witi Ihimaera, Kahu's great-grandfather is the chief of his community and he was disappointed when Kahu was born that she wasn't a boy. He looks for possible future leaders among the boys in the community. He teaches them Maori skills and sets them special tasks. In one of these tasks, he takes the boys out on the sea in a boat and throws a special stone into the water. The boys have to dive down, find the stone and bring it back. But none of them can do it. Kahu's great-grandfather is very disappointed and sad about this. Kahu loves her great-grandather, who she calls 'Paka', and she wants to make him happy. So the next morning, when Kahu's uncle Rawiri is taking his boat out, she asks if she can go with him. Kahu's great-grandmother, Nani Flowers, goes with them too. She knows the place where the stone was thrown into the water.

---

3 What do the verbs in each group have in common? Find them in the story and, with a partner, try to work out their meaning. Use a dictionary to help you.

Group 1

do a duck dive *(line 12)*
dog paddle *(line 19)*
float *(line 20)*
drown *(line 24)*
drift *(line 41)*
tread water *(line 66)*

Group 2

scream *(line 7)*
yell *(line 10)*
sob *(line 69)*
cry *(line 35)*

Group 3

jab *(line 7)*
push *(line 9)*
throw *(line 11)*
wave *(line 17)*
grab *(line 28)*
point *(line 38)*

Group 4

gasp *(line 21)*
swallow *(line 21)*
cough *(line 22)*
splutter *(line 22)*

4 Find the following in the extract.

1 an example of humour
2 an example of exaggeration (where something is made to seem more than it really is)
3 two or three images which create a picture in the reader's mind

5 Work with a partner. Discuss these questions.

1 Who is the comic character in this extract?
2 Why does the writer use humour here? Does it add drama?
3 How does the writer build suspense?
4 What do you learn about Kahu from this extract?

The Whale Rider

Kahu said simply, "I'll get it."

Before we could stop her she stood up and dived overboard. Until that moment I had never even known that she could swim.

5 Nani's mouth made a big 'O'. Then the breath rushed into her lungs and she screamed, "Oh, no!" She jabbed me hard and said, "Go after her, Rawiri, *Go.*" She virtually pushed me over the side of the rowboat.

10 "Give me the diving mask," I yelled. Nani Flowers threw it at me and quickly I put it on. I took three deep breaths and did a duck dive.

I couldn't see her. The sea looked empty. There was only a small stingray flapping 15 down towards the reef.

Then I got a big fright because the stingray turned around and, smiling, waved at me. It was Kahu in her white dress and sandals, dog paddling down to the sea floor, her 20 braids floating around her head.

I gasped and swallowed sea water. I came to the surface coughing and spluttering.

"Where is she!" Nani Flowers screamed. "Has she drowned? Oh, no, my Kahu." And 25 before I could stop her she jumped in beside me, just about emptying the whole ocean. She didn't even give me a chance to explain as she grabbed the mask off me and put it on. Then she tried to swim underwater, but her dress 30 was so filled with air that no matter how hard she tried she remained on the surface like a balloon with legs kicking out of it. I doubt if she could have gotten deeper anyway because she was so fat she couldn't sink.

35 "Oh, Kahu," Nani Flowers cried again. But this time I told her to take a deep breath and, when she was looking underwater, to watch where I would point.

We went beneath the surface. Suddenly I 40 pointed down. Kahu was searching the reef, drifting around the coral. Nani Flowers' eyes widened with disbelief.

Whatever it was Kahu was searching for, she was having difficulty finding it. But just then

45 white shapes came speeding out of the dark towards her. I thought they were sharks, and Nani Flowers began to blow bubbles of terror.

They were dolphins. They circled around Kahu and seemed to be talking to her. She 50 nodded and grabbed one around its body. As quick as a flash, the dolphins sped her to another area of the reef and stopped. Kahu seemed to say, "Down here?" and the dolphins made a nodding motion.

55 Suddenly Kahu made a quick darting gesture. She picked something up, inspected it, appeared satisfied with it, and went back to the dolphins. Slowly the girl and the dolphins rose towards us. But just as they 60 were midway, Kahu stopped again. She kissed the dolphins goodbye and gave Nani Flowers a heart attack by returning to the reef. She picked up a crayfish and resumed her upward journey. The dolphins were like 65 silver dreams as they disappeared.

Nani Flowers and I were treading water when Kahu appeared between us, smoothing her hair back from her face and blinking away the sea water. Nani Flowers, sobbing, 70 hugged her close in the water.

"I'm all right, Nani," Kahu laughed.

She showed the crayfish to us. "This is for Paka's tea," she said. "And you can give him back his stone."

75 She placed the stone in Nani Flowers' hands.

by Witi Ihimaera

braids (*line 20*) *American English* hair twisted together in a pattern (they are called 'plaits' – pronounced 'plats' – in British English)

Review of Units 7–8

Vocabulary

Kitchen appliances and equipment

1 Write the names of the kitchen appliances and equipment.

1 It heats food very quickly. *microwave*
2 It's a machine that washes plates and dishes.
3 You keep frozen food in it.
4 It keeps food cold.
5 You use them to weigh ingredients.
6 It makes toast.
7 You cook stir-fried dishes in it.
8 You make tea in it.
9 It's an electrical appliance. It gets warm when you switch it on and you use it on your clothes.
10 Put a banana, some sugar and some milk in it. Switch it on and make a banana milkshake.

2 Complete the captions.

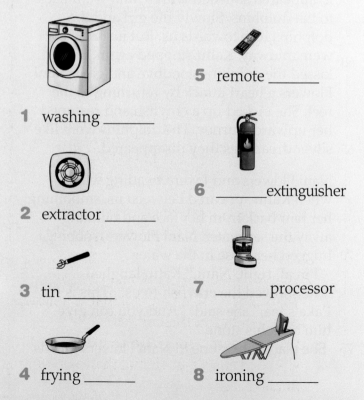

1 washing _____
2 extractor _____
3 tin _____
4 frying _____
5 remote _____
6 _____extinguisher
7 _____ processor
8 ironing _____

Use of English

3 Complete the sentences with the words from the box.

| away   on   off   up |

1 I can't hear the TV. Would you mind turning it _____?
2 When you leave the room, please switch the lights _____ to save electricity.
3 There's some soup in the fridge. You can heat it _____ in the microwave.
4 Don't worry if you're in a hurry. I'll wash _____.
5 Could you put the food processor _____ when you've finished with it?
6 Put the light _____ if you can't see to read.

4 Complete the second sentence so that it means the same as the first. Use the words in brackets.

1 I'm nowhere near as practical as you.
You're <u>much more practical than me</u>.
(*much*)
2 The film is nowhere near as interesting as the book.
The book is _____.
(*far*)
3 Your room is much more colourful than mine.
My room _____.
(*nowhere near as ... as*)
4 Seoul is far busier than London.
London is _____
_____. (*a lot less*)
5 The metro in Zurich is far more expensive than the metro in Vienna.
The metro in Vienna is _____
_____. (*much*)

5 Complete this text about glucose using the verbs in brackets. Remember to use the present passive.

Glucose

- Glucose *is produced*[1] by carbon dioxide, water and sunlight. (*produce*)
- It _____[2] by cells for aerobic respiration. (*need*)
- In this process, glucose and oxygen _____[3] into carbon dioxide and water. (*change*)
- Glucose _____[4] at night. (*not produce*)

6 Change these active sentences into passive sentences without *by*.

1 Someone has found my watch.
My watch has been found.

2 Someone has left a bag in the classroom.
_____

3 Someone hasn't turned the lights off.
_____

4 Someone has tidied my room!
_____

5 People have told me that I look like my father.
_____

7 Change these active sentences into passive sentences with *by*.

1 My sports teacher has asked me to play for the team.
I've been asked to play for the team by my
sports teacher.

2 My aunt has given me a gold necklace.
I _____.

3 People all over the world have watched the Olympic Games.
The Olympic Games _____
_____.

4 A famous director has made the book into a film.
The book _____
_____.

5 The headteacher has asked us to sing in assembly.
We _____.

General knowledge quiz

8 Work with a partner. Ask and answer the questions.

1 Which is the largest rainforest in the world?

2 Name four things from the rainforests that we eat and drink.

3 Why are trees good for the environment?

4 Look at the diagram. What is this process called?

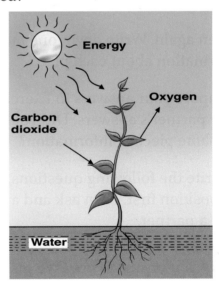

5 In which country is Nairobi National Park?

6 Name three animals that live in Nairobi National Park.

7 What is a predator? Give an example.

8 What do you call an animal that is hunted and eaten by another animal?

9 What is a herbivore? Give an example.

10 What do you call an animal that eats other animals?

9 Buildings and structures

- **Topics** Famous buildings; a famous bridge; a design for a school
- **Use of English** Questions beginning with prepositions; past continuous active and passive

Brilliant buildings

[handwritten notes: 1. 圣索菲亚大教堂 / 1. 阿拉伯塔 / 2. Colosseum [ˌkɒləˈsiːəm] / (ˈmʌdʒ ˈsɪəm) 角斗场]

- How many famous buildings can you think of? Do they have anything in common?

Reading and speaking

1 Work with a partner. Take turns to ask and answer the questions in the quiz on page 73.

Listening 🔘 19

2 Listen and check your answers.

3 Listen again. Write down one more piece of information about each place.

4 Compare your answers to Exercise 3 with your partner's answers. Did you write down the same piece of information?

5 Rewrite the following questions, putting the preposition first. Then ask and answer them with a partner.

1 Which city is the Empire State Building in?
2 Which country did Marco Polo set sail from on his travels to Asia?
3 Which Spanish island is Mount Teide on?
4 Which country did the Portuguese explorer, Vasco da Gama, sail to in 1498?
5 Who did the French give the Statue of Liberty to in 1886?

Use of English: Questions beginning with prepositions

It's sometimes clearer to put the preposition at the beginning of a question.

In which country is the ancient city of Petra?
sounds better than
Which country is the ancient city of Petra in?

From which building can you watch the sun set twice in less than a minute?
sounds better than
Which building can you watch the sun set twice in less than a minute from?

General knowledge quiz

1 In which ancient ruined city are you standing if you can see the Andes mountains?
   a Ur, in Iraq
   b Machu Picchu, in Peru
   c Petra, in Jordan

2 From which building can you see the Eiffel Tower?
   a the Colosseum, in Rome
   b the Kremlin, in Moscow
   c the Louvre Museum, in Paris

3 For whom was the Taj Mahal built? It was built ...
   a for Shah Jahan, in memory of his third wife.
   b for Shah Jahan, to celebrate his wedding.
   c for Genghis Khan, as a palace.

4 In which country is the ancient city of Petra?
   a Italy
   b Jordan
   c Malaysia

5 In which city is Al-Masjid al-Haram, the biggest mosque in the world?
   a Istanbul
   b Mecca
   c Cairo

6 For which event was the Beijing National Stadium built?
   a the 2010 World Cup
   b the 2009 Asian Games
   c the 2008 Olympic Games

7 From which building can you watch the sun set twice in less than a minute?
   a the Eiffel Tower in Paris
   b the Burj Khalifa building in Dubai
   c the CN Tower in Toronto, Canada

8 On which building does the sun cast a shadow like a snake at the spring equinox?
   a the Great Pyramid at Giza, in Egypt
   b the Pyramid of El Castillo at Chichén Itzá in Mexico
   c the temple of Angkor Wat in Cambodia

9 On which building is there a roof designed to look like the sails on a ship?
   a the Sydney Opera House in Sydney, Australia
   b the Parthenon in Athens, Greece
   c the Sagrada Familia cathedral in Barcelona, Spain

10 To which city do you go if you want to see the Alhambra Palace?
   a Granada, in the south of Spain
   b Marrakech, in Morocco
   c Ankara, in Turkey

Art meets engineering

- How many bridges can you think of within ten kilometres of where you are now? What are they made of? Why are they there?

1 Match the types of bridge with their definitions.

1 suspension bridge *b*
2 viaduct *d*
3 aqueduct *e*
4 footbridge *f*
5 drawbridge *c*
6 cable-stayed bridge *a*

a It has towers from which cables are hung to support the deck.
b It is supported by strong steel cables hung from a tower at each end of the bridge.
c Castles and old cities had this type of moveable bridge.
d It carries vehicles, such as trains and cars, over a valley.
e It carries water.
f It's a narrow bridge for pedestrians.

Reading

2 Read the text. What makes the Millau Viaduct different from other bridges?

The Millau Viaduct in France is a cable-stayed bridge. It is Europe's highest bridge, 270 metres above the River Tarn at its highest point and 2,460 metres long. The tallest pylon is 343 metres above the valley. The bridge is unusual because it is not straight: it has a slight curve and it is gently sloping. It is supported by seven columns which are called 'piers'. The deck of the bridge has four lanes for traffic, two in each direction.

While the piers were being built across the valley, the deck of the bridge was being constructed on the land at each end of the viaduct. The deck was then rolled across from one pier to the next. In total, the bridge took three years to build. It was finished ahead of schedule and within budget. Building bridges is a dangerous occupation. When the Sydney Harbour Bridge was being built, for example, 16 workers died. When the Millau Viaduct was being built, no one was killed.

Soon after the bridge opened to traffic, cars were stopping in the safety lane so that the drivers and passengers could see the view from the bridge. Clearly, this is dangerous, so now people have to use the viewing points before or after crossing.

3 Decide whether these statements about the Millau Viaduct are true or false.

1 It's a footbridge.
2 You could go under it if you were going down the River Tarn.
3 There aren't many bridges like it.
4 The piers of the bridge were completed before the deck was built.
5 It took longer to build than people had expected.
6 It cost more to build than people had expected.
7 It had a better safety record than the Sydney Harbour Bridge.
8 There are places on the bridge where you can stop and see the view.

4 Complete the sentences using the verbs in brackets. Remember to use the past continuous passive.

1 We couldn't use our classroom last week because it was _being repainted_. (repaint)
2 I couldn't get my emails because my computer was _____. (repair)
3 We couldn't go swimming because the pool was _____ for a competition. (use)
4 We arrived at the match just as the names of the players _____. (announce)
5 I felt really nervous on stage when I realised I _____ by so many people! (watch)
6 You played really well in the concert. You didn't know you _____, did you? (record)

Writing and speaking

5 Find out about another bridge and complete a fact file for it. Try to find out about something that happened while it was being built and add this to your fact file.

6 Give a short presentation to the class about the bridge you have chosen.

Use of English: Past continuous, active and passive

Use the past continuous to say that something **was happening** around a particular time in the past.

Past continuous active

| was / were | verb + -ing |

Soon after the bridge opened to traffic, cars were stopping in the safety lane so that the drivers and passengers could see the view from the bridge.

Past continuous passive

| was / were being | past participle |

While the piers were being built across the valley, the deck of the bridge was being constructed on the land at each end of the viaduct.

When the Millau Viaduct was being built, no one was killed.

Language tip

Use tall for people, trees, buildings and for things that are higher than they are wide.

How **tall** are you?

The **tallest** pylon is 343 metres above the valley.

Use high for other things, such as mountains and bridges.

How **high** is Kilimanjaro?

It's the **highest** bridge in the world.

A new look at school design

- With a partner, ask and answer the following questions in relation to your own school.

1 Is there enough space in and around the school?
2 What are the noise levels like?
3 Does it fit in with the local environment?
4 Are there good views from the classrooms?
5 Is there enough natural light?
6 What safety features are there?

1 The plan below shows the design for a new school. Work with a partner. Look at it carefully. What do you think of it?

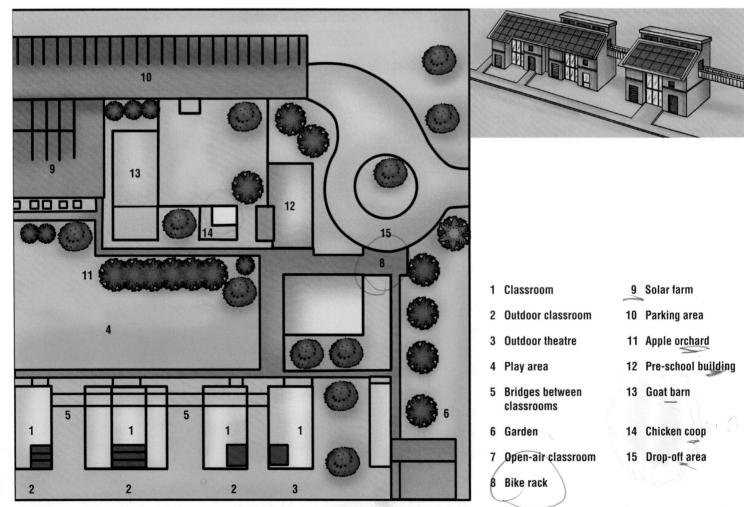

1	Classroom	9	Solar farm
2	Outdoor classroom	10	Parking area
3	Outdoor theatre	11	Apple orchard
4	Play area	12	Pre-school building
5	Bridges between classrooms	13	Goat barn
6	Garden	14	Chicken coop
7	Open-air classroom	15	Drop-off area
8	Bike rack		

Reading

2 Complete the text using the words from the box and referring to the school plan in Exercise 1.

open-air classroom	parking
bridges	classrooms
goat barn	outdoor classrooms
solar farm	

The school buildings have two storeys. The classrooms[1] are all on the ground floor. There are lofts above each classroom where teachers and students can store equipment, books, materials and their work. Staircases lead to the loft, from which students can look down to their classrooms. Students go from one classroom to another by walking across the ....[2] between the buildings. There are views from the windows across the surrounding countryside.

All the indoor classrooms have access to the ....[3], which are used when the weather is fine. There is also an ....[4] near the garden. The school is heated by solar energy provided by its own ....[5].

Other features include a vegetable garden, an apple orchard, a ....[6] and a chicken coop.

The school is convenient for parents who can drop off their children outside the pre-school building. There is also a large ....[7] area.

Project: Design your ideal school

3 Work in small groups.

1 Decide on a location.
2 Decide what the building should look like.
3 Decide on the facilities. You can include some of the facilities from the plan on page 76 and any others you think are important.
4 Decide who's going to do each task.

I think it should be in / near ...

I think it should be a two-storey building. It should have lots of natural light ...

I think it should have ...

Who's going to draw the plan?

I'll do the key, if you like.

Will you write the description?

Design and shape

- **Topics** Shopping for food; three-dimensional shapes; classic designs
- **Use of English** Quantifiers with countable and uncountable nouns (*a bar of, a slice of,* etc.)

A bar of chocolate

- Do you enjoy shopping for food? Why? Why not?

Listening 20

1 Listen. Where is William going and why?

2 Listen again. Write the shopping list. Write down the items but not the quantities.

bread, cold meat, biscuits, ...

Language tip

a couple of = two

Use of English: Quantifiers with countable and uncountable nouns

You can use the expressions below when you want to specify a certain amount of something.

a bar of chocolate	a box of matches
a loaf of bread	a jar of jam, olives
a slice of cake, cheese, meat	a carton of yoghurt, milk
a packet of biscuits, noodles, rice	a bottle of water
a bunch of flowers, bananas	a can of cola
	a tin of soup, tomatoes
	a bag of crisps

---

3 Look at the *Use of English* box. Which of the phrases in red

1 mean 'a container of'?

2 contain a unit noun meaning 'a piece of'?

3 contain a group noun meaning 'a set of'?

4 Work with a partner. Describe the items in the shopping basket at the top of the page.

5 Use the quantifiers in the *Use of English* box to describe each of the following.

1 a slice of toast

6 Listen again. Write down exactly what William had to buy at the supermarket. Use the correct quantifiers.

two loaves of bread, ...

Language tip

Singular	Plural
one loaf	two loaves

Speaking

7 Work with a partner. Roleplay the conversation between William and his mother. Use the list you wrote in Exercise 6 to help you.

A *Here's the shopping list.*

B *Right. Bread, how much bread?*

8 Play this chain game around the class.

A *I went to the supermarket and I bought a packet of rice.*

B *I went to the supermarket and I bought a packet of rice and a loaf of bread.*

C *I went to the supermarket and I bought a packet of rice, a loaf of bread and a ...*

What shape is it?

- How many shapes can you see around you now?
  (Rectangles? Squares? Circles? Triangles?)

Vocabulary

1 Match the words to the 3D (three-dimensional) shapes.

sphere

cube

cylinder

triangular prism

hexagonal prism

square-based pyramid

triangular pyramid

hemisphere

cone

1

2

3

4

5

6

7

8

9

2 A 'net' is a pattern that you can cut and fold to make a 3D shape.
Match these nets to the shapes in Exercise 1.

1 *a cube*

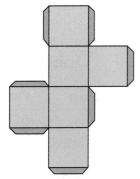

2

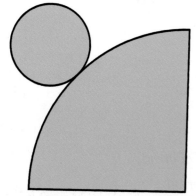

3

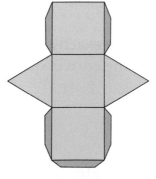

4

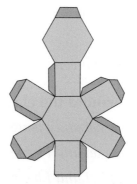

Listening 21

3 Listen to an extract from a radio programme. What is it about? Who is it for?

4 Listen again. The presenters give examples to illustrate what they're talking about. Write them in a list.

cube: an ice cube, ...

5 How many of the items on your list can you see in the mystery photos?

Speaking

6 Work with a partner. The presenter says that a lot of candles are cylindrical – in the shape of a cylinder. She also says that candles come in a lot of shapes. Can you think of any more?

Candles can be ...

I've seen a candle that was in the shape of a ...

7 In pairs, ask and answer these questions.
1 Why is the ball used in games such as football, table tennis and golf a sphere?
2 Why is a can of cola cylindrical?
3 Why is ice cream often served in a cone?
4 Why are traffic cones in the shape of a cone?
5 Why is ice made in cubes?

Classic designs

- Give an example of an everyday object which you think is well designed. What's good about its design?

Reading

1 Look at the pictures. To which two objects do these descriptions refer?

This piece of furniture takes its name from a city in Mexico. It was first produced in the 1950s. It was designed to keep you cool while you're sitting down. It's usually made of vinyl cords on a metal, pear-shaped frame. It is very comfortable.

This was designed in Germany in the 1930s by Ferdinand Porsche. It was very popular because it was practical and it wasn't expensive. It gets its nickname, the Beetle, from its unusual shape. It has been manufactured and used around the world for 80 years. It's been everything from a taxi to a fashion icon!

Listening (22)

2 Listen to four more descriptions. Match them to the photos.

3 Listen again. What are the reasons for the success of the objects described?

Speaking

4 Work in pairs. Say what you like or don't like about each of the objects in the photos. Use the words below.

- comfortable
- practical
- (not) expensive
- unusual
- simple
- beautiful
- attractive

Reading

5 Read about Eva Valicsek's design. What materials did she use?

Hungarian design student Eva Valicsek, has designed the egg carton of the future. It's made of cardboard and a rubber band.

"As a starting point, I wanted to design a flexible box to fit different egg sizes," she says. She made a lot of models to find the right design. Then she found the perfect solution by using a simple rubber band. Unlike existing egg boxes, Eva's carton can hold either small eggs or large eggs equally well. The eggs are held firmly in the carton, thanks to the flexible rubber band and the cut-out holes. It is also open at the top, which means you can see what you're buying.

Eva's egg carton is environmentally friendly because it can be reused many times.

Source: www.bbc.com

Speaking

6 List the advantages of Eva's design.

It's simple to make.

Project: Design a product

7 You're going to work in groups on a design. Choose one of the following:

● a new type of cover to protect your mobile phone
● a new type of footwear
● a new type of car

1 Decide on the features of your product that will make it new and special. Write a list.

2 Ask one or two people in the group to draw a picture of the product.

3 Comment on the picture and make any changes that are necessary.

4 Write a description of the product.
  ● Say what advantages your product has.
  ● Say why it is different from existing products.
  ● Say what it is made of.

5 Present your product to the rest of the class.

Poetry

The Canadian poet Elizabeth Brewster started writing poetry when she was a child. Her first poem was published when she was 12.

1 What do you know about the climate of Canada?

2 Read the poem. Where does the writer come from?

Where I come from

People are made of places. They carry with them
hints of jungles or mountains, a tropic grace
or the cool eyes of sea-gazers. Atmosphere of cities
how different drops from them, like the smell of smog
5 or the almost-not-smell of tulips in the spring,
nature tidily plotted in little squares
with a fountain in the centre; museum smell,
art also tidily plotted with a guidebook;
or the smell of work, glue factories maybe,
10 chromium-plated offices; smell of subways
crowded at rush hours.

Where I come from, people
carry woods in their minds, acres of pine woods;
blueberry patches in the burned-out bush;
15 wooden farmhouses, old, in need of paint,
with yards where hens and chickens circle about,
clucking aimlessly; battered schoolhouses
behind which violets grow. Spring and winter
are the mind's chief season: ice and the breaking of ice.

20 A door in the mind blows open, and there blows
a frosty wind from fields of snow.

by Elizabeth Brewster

hints *(line 2)* suggestions

tropic *(line 2)* (tropical) from the areas near the equator

grace *(line 2)* the quality of moving in a smooth, attractive way

sea-gazers *(line 3)* people who look at the sea for a long time

smog *(line 4)* air pollution produced by smoke, gases and chemicals

tulips *(line 5)* brightly coloured spring flowers in the shape of a cup

plotted *(line 6)* placed on a map

glue *(line 9)* a substance used to stick things to together

chromium-plated *(line 10)* covered with chromium, a white metal

acres *(line 13)* measured areas of land (1 acre = 4,047 square metres)

clucking *(line 17)* making a noise that a chicken makes

aimlessly *(line 17)* with no purpose or plan

battered *(line 17)* old and not in very good condition

violets *(line 18)* small plants with small purple flowers

3 **Work in pairs. Discuss these questions.**

1 Read the first three lines of the poem again, from 'People ... ' to '... sea-gazers'. What is the purpose of these three lines?

2 Read the rest of the first verse, from 'Atmosphere of cities ... ' to ' ... crowded at rush hours'. How does the author feel about cities?

3 Read the second verse. How does the author feel about where she comes from?

4 Read the last verse. What do you think it means?

4 **What do you think the following lines from the poem mean?**

1 'art also tidily plotted with a guidebook' *(line 8)*

2 'people / carry woods in their minds' *(lines 12–13)*

3 'Spring and winter / are the mind's chief seasons: ice and the breaking of ice' *(lines 18–19)* (Think of the climate where the author lived.)

5 **Work in groups. Read the poem again. Then close your books. How many images (pictures) from the poem can you remember? Write them down. Then compare your lists with the lists of other groups.**

6 **Write an analysis of the poem. Use this guide to help you.**

- In the first three lines of the poem, the author introduces ...
- The rest of verse one describes ....
- The second verse describes ...
- The last two lines of the poem ...
- There are some very striking images in the poem, for example:
- The poem illustrates very well how 'people are made of places'.

Review Units 9–10

Vocabulary

Types of bridge

 1 Label the bridges.

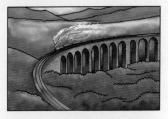
a

b

c

d

e

| suspension bridge | viaduct | aqueduct |
| footbridge | drawbridge | |

2 Complete the words. Then match them to the diagrams.

1 c _o_ _n_ _e_   a

2 c__b__   b

3 cyl__nd__r   c

4 sph__r__   d

5 h__x__g__n__l prism   e

6 h__m__sph__r__   f

7 squ__r__-based pyramid g

8 tr__ __ng__l__r prism h

9 tr__ __ng__l__r pyr__m__d i

Use of English

3 Use the prompts to write questions for these answers. Start each one with a preposition.

1 Q: city / the White House / ? *In which city is the White House?*
A: It's in Washington DC.

2 Q: island / Mount Fuji / ?
A: It's on Honshu Island.

3 Q: river / Tower Bridge / ?
A: It's over the Thames in London.

4 Q: city / the volcano Popocatépetl / ?
A: You can see it from Mexico City.

5 Q: Italian city / Marco Polo / in 1271 / ?
A: He sailed from Venice.

6 Q: ocean / the Amazon river / ?
A: It flows into the Atlantic.

4 Rewrite the underlined part of each sentence using the passive. Add *by* + noun if you need to say who was doing the action.

1 We couldn't go over the bridge because <u>they were repairing it</u>.

it was being repaired

2 We couldn't use the swimming pool because <u>they were cleaning it</u>.

3 I woke up because <u>someone was calling me</u>.

4 The traffic had to go through the town while <u>they were building the bridge</u>.

5 You didn't look nervous during the performance even though <u>everyone was watching you</u>.

6 My brother didn't realise that <u>the cat was following him</u>.

5 Write the missing words.

1 a _____ of chocolate

2 a _____ of bread

3 a _____ of cheese

4 a _____ of eggs

5 a _____ of rice

6 a _____ of grapes

7 a _____ of tissues

8 a _____ of honey

9 a _____ of water

10 a _____ of cola

General knowledge quiz

6 Work with a partner. Ask and answer the questions.

1 Which cities do you associate with the following?
  a the Alhambra Palace
  b the Eiffel Tower
  c the CN Tower

2 In which country is the ancient city of Ur?

3 What is this and where is it?

4 It's Europe's highest bridge and it's above the River Tarn in France. What's it called?

5 How many sides does a hexagon have?

6 What is this car called and who designed it?

7 For which event was the Beijing National Stadium built?

8 Where is the temple of Angkor Wat?

9 What's the difference between a viaduct and an aqueduct?

10 It's a classic chair that takes its name from a city in Mexico. What is it?

11 Personality types

- **Topics** Aspects of personality; profile of a young inventor; soap opera
- **Use of English** Adjectives followed by prepositions; prepositions followed by nouns; abstract nouns

What are you really like?

- Describe yourself using three adjectives.

Vocabulary

1 Choose the adjectives from the list to describe a good friend.

adventurous   generous   logical   pessimistic

calm   **hard-working**   modest   loyal   quick-tempered

cautious   honest   optimistic   shy   sociable

decisive   impatient   **organised**   spontaneous

determined   independent

easy-going   kind   patient   sympathetic

2 How many pairs of opposites can you find in Exercise 1? Make a list.

Reading

3 Work with a partner. Do the personality test on page 87 using the instructions below.

1 Student A: For each of the statements, choose one of the options: *I strongly agree, I disagree,* etc. Tell your partner the number of points you get for each statement.
Student B: Write down the number of points Student A gets for each statement, like this:

Part A	Part B	Part C	Part D
1	5		
2	3		

2 Student B: Add up the scores for each part of the test. Then use the *Analysis* to tell Student A what sort of personality he or she has. Does he / she agree?
3 Change roles.

4 Rewrite the sentences in the *Use of English* box so that they're true for you.

Use of English: Adjectives followed by prepositions

Adjectives sometimes have prepositions after them. It's helpful to learn them as whole phrases.

I'm *interested in* people.

I'm *good at* practical things.

I'm *aware of* what I can and can't do.

It's sometimes *difficult for* me to tell people the truth if I think it will upset them.

Friendship is very *important to* me.

I get *upset about* last-minute changes to plans.

I get *annoyed with* people who aren't sensible and practical.

Personality test

Options:

I strongly disagree = 1 point

I disagree = 2 points

I'm not sure = 3 points

I agree = 4 points

I strongly agree = 5 points

	Part A	Points
1	I like being with people.	
2	I'm more interested in people than in their ideas.	
3	I'm very sociable and I have a lot of friends.	
4	I'm popular with people of my own age.	
5	Being with other people cheers me up if I'm feeling sad.	
	Score for Part A:__	

	Part B	Points
1	I'm a logical person.	
2	I'm good at practical things.	
3	I'm aware of what I can and can't do.	
4	I like dealing with facts.	
5	I need to see the evidence before I believe something is true.	
	Score for Part B:__	

	Part C	Points
1	Before I make a decision, I think carefully about it.	
2	I think you should always speak the truth, even if it's difficult for someone to hear.	
3	I get annoyed with people who aren't sensible and practical.	
4	I like people who can make decisions.	
5	I like to be in control of what I'm doing.	
	Score for Part C:__	

	Part D	Points
1	I always know where everything is.	
2	It's important to me to be on time with my work.	
3	I like to know exactly what I'm doing and when.	
4	I get upset about last-minute changes to plans.	
5	I'm always on time.	
	Score for Part D:__	

Analysis

Score	Part A	Part B	Part C	Part D
5–14	Cautious	Creative	Sympathetic	Spontaneous
15–25	Sociable	Realistic	Decisive	Organised

A teenage millionaire

- What are the qualities you need to be successful?

Reading

1 Read this news story. Why is the title 'App-solutely amazing!'?

App-solutely amazing!

Nick D'Aloisio got his first laptop when he was nine. He started designing apps when he was 12 and at 15 he launched an iPhone app called 'Summly'. It was an app which summarised stories in the news and it was downloaded by nearly a million people. His app has recently been bought by an Internet giant for $30 million.

"The proudest moment for me has been seeing these tweets coming through from teenagers saying, 'You've inspired me.' I'm so excited about that," says Nick.

His mother says she was never worried about the amount of time he was spending on the computer, "because he would always show us what he was doing. I remember him creating 3D models on his computer as a 10-year-old."

Nick isn't a stereotypical computer nerd. Nor is he arrogant and self-centred, which you might expect of a boy who has been described as a 'genius'. He is polite, likeable, enthusiastic and self-aware.

He enjoys the humanities, cricket and rugby. "I want to do Philosophy at university and I'm studying Chinese and Russian at school," he says. He doesn't want to work in computer programming. He's more interested in product design.

What's he going to do with the money from his app? He might buy some clothes, he says, and maybe a new computer. One thing he'd like to do is to invest in small companies. "That's what is exciting, and if you are lucky to have a bit of money, you can take those risks. That's what I would do if I was going to go and spend it."

What is Summly?

"It helps publishers reach out to a younger audience," Nick says. He feels that young people are interested in the news, but they don't want to spend a lot of time reading long stories if they're not relevant to their lives. With Summly, you quickly find out whether a story might be interesting.

Source: The Guardian

Vocabulary

2 Read the article again and make a list of all the personality adjectives. Which qualities are positive (+) and which are negative (–)?

arrogant (–)

3 Match the words to their definitions.

1 launched
2 summarised
3 proudest
4 inspired
5 stereotypical
6 nerd (*informal*)
7 genius
8 the humanities
9 invest in
10 take risks

a described briefly the main facts or ideas
b do something which may not be successful and may even be dangerous
c give money to a business, usually in order to make a profit
d happiest because of something you have achieved
e having the qualities that you expect a particular type of person to have
f made a product available for the first time
g made someone feel they want to do something and can do it
h someone who is extremely intelligent or good at doing something
i someone, especially a boy or a man, who is not fashionable and who is interested in boring things
j subjects that are not connected with science (such as History and Languages)

Speaking

4 Work with a partner. Ask and answer the questions.

1 What did Nick do when he was 15?
2 What is Summly?
3 Has Summly been successful? How do you know?
4 What is Nick most pleased about?
5 What's he like as a person?
6 What are his plans?

> **Use of English: Prepositions followed by nouns**
>
> Nouns sometimes have prepositions before them. It's helpful to learn them as whole phrases.

5 Find these expressions in the newspaper story about Nick D'Aloisio.

- *at* 15
- *at* university
- *at* school
- *in* the news
- *on* his computer

6 Complete these sentences with the correct preposition: *in*, *on* or *at*.

1 Nick is still ____ school.
2 ____ the moment he's studying Chinese and Russian.
3 This is a brilliant app ____ my opinion.
4 Has Nick been ____ TV?
5 He looks quite young ____ the photo.
6 He likes being ____ control of what he's doing.
7 He doesn't want a job ____ computer programming.
8 You can read news stories ____ your phone.
9 I read the story ____ the Internet.
10 He lives ____ home with his parents and his younger brother.

Writing

7 Write a summary of the news story in Exercise 1 for Nick's Summly website. Use your answers to the questions in Exercise 4 as a guide. Don't write more than 50 words.

The world of soap opera

● What is a soap opera?

Listening 23

1 Listen to this radio programme. What is the topic of the discussion?

2 Listen again and answer the questions.
1 How would you summarise Karim's opinion?
2 How would you summarise Melina's opinion?
3 Can you tell what the interviewer's opinion is?

3 Listen again. Listen for the abstract nouns corresponding to these adjectives. Write them down. Use a dictionary to check your spelling.

Adjective	Noun
jealous	*jealousy*
greedy	
ambitious	
afraid	
angry	
loyal	
brave	

4 Use a dictionary to find the abstract nouns corresponding to these adjectives.

1 generous   *generosity*
2 optimistic
3 patient
4 independent
5 kind
6 modest
7 shy
8 enthusiastic
9 arrogant

> **Use of English: Abstract nouns**
>
> Words like *jealousy* and *greed* are abstract nouns. We usually use abstract nouns without *the* or *a*.
>
> There is often an adjective which comes from the abstract noun.
>
> *jealousy*   *jealous*
>
> *greed*   *greedy*

Speaking

5 Work in groups. Think of a soap opera that's popular in your country and answer the questions.

1 Who are the main characters?
2 How would you describe their personalities?
3 Which emotions feature most frequently?

Project: A description of a soap opera

6 Write a description of a popular soap opera for a website about TV programmes.

1 Answer these questions.
   ● What's it called?
   ● Where and when is it set?
   ● Who are the main characters and what are they like?
2 Describe one or two of the major events in the story.
3 Illustrate your description with a photo from the series.

- **Topics** Jobs and places of work; talking about jobs; future predictions
- **Use of English** Suffixes for job titles; verbs and prepositions followed by verb + *-ing*; *will* future and future continuous

The world of work

- What's your ideal job?

Vocabulary

1 Match the jobs to the people in the picture.

-ist	-or	-er	-ic	-ant	-ian	other
dentist	doctor	cleaner	paramedic	shop assistant	optician	chef
receptionist	driving	firefighter	car mechanic		electrician	engineer
physiotherapist	instructor	taxi driver				nurse
pharmacist		carpenter				traffic
		plumber				warden
		police officer				
		manager				
		waiter/waitress				

Street

Listening (24)

2 Listen to people talking about their work. What jobs do you think they do?

3 Listen again. Who talks about the following?

1 working at a football club
2 meeting interesting people
3 life-and-death situations
4 working inside and outside
5 dealing with difficult customers
6 having their own business

4 Add the correct suffixes to the words to make job titles.

1 music *musician*
2 write
3 farm work
4 act
5 journal

6 build
7 direct
8 garden
9 design
10 (flight) attend

Speaking

5 Work in groups. Talk about the people you know and the jobs they do.

> **Use of English: Suffixes for job titles**
>
> A suffix is a group of letters at the end of a word. Several job titles end in common suffixes, such as *-ist, -er, -ian, -ic, -ant, -or.*
>
> drive (*verb*) driver (*noun*)
>
> physiotherapy (*noun for the activity*) physiotherapist (*noun for the person who does the job*)
>
> electric (*adjective*), electricity (*noun*) electrician (*noun for the person who works with electricity*)

Language tip

If you're not sure how to describe a person's job title, you can say:

He / She **works in** *marketing / computing / finance / advertising / publishing,* etc.

You can also say:

He / She **works in** *a shop.*

He / She **works for** *a pharmaceutical company.*

> My mum works in banking.

> My dad's a sales manager. He works for an import and export company.

A day in the life

- To be a firefighter, what kind of person do you need to be?

Reading

1 Read this description of a typical day in the life of a firefighter. Is there anything that surprises you?

Butler Fire Station is in Perth in north-west Australia. The firefighters are volunteers. At the fire station, there are regular duties to be performed, as well as responding to emergencies. The firefighters need to be ready to go in 90 seconds at any time.

A typical day

8.00–8.30	We start by checking the equipment. You can't risk taking out equipment or machinery that doesn't work.
8.30–9.30	We all have to spend an hour in the gym doing strength and fitness training. Sometimes I don't feel like working out, but we have to do it to keep fit.
10.00–12.00	Morning duties. This involves going out into the community, and it includes checking hydrants, going on school visits, and doing building inspections. When we've finished doing our community work, we practise cutting open cars and things like that.
12.00–13.00	Lunch. We all enjoy sitting down and having a break for lunch, but we know that we might be called out to an emergency at any moment.
13.00–13.30	Station duties. This means cleaning the station. I don't mind doing this, but it's not the most exciting part of the job!
13.30–16.00	Training and inspections (similar to morning duties).
16.00–17.00	Study and/or gym. In this job, you have to keep on learning. One of the challenges of working as a firefighter is keeping up with new technology. I'm interested in finding out how things work, so that's OK. **Before leaving, we make sure the people working on the next shift are ready to take over.**

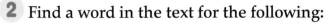

Vocabulary

2 Find a word in the text for the following:

1 people who do work without being paid, especially work that involves helping people *volunteers*
2 things you have to do as part of your job
3 serious or dangerous situations that need immediate action
4 the people living in a particular area

5 pipes at the side of the road, connected to the water system, and used to get water to stop fires
6 a careful look at something, to check, for example, that it is working properly
7 a period of work, in a place such as a factory or a hospital
8 to start being responsible for something

3 Read the text again. What does the firefighter feel about the different aspects of her job? What does she enjoy? What isn't she so keen on?

Use of English: Verbs and prepositions followed by verb + *-ing*

After some verbs, we use the *-ing* form of the verb, not an infinitive.

We also use the *-ing* form after all prepositions, e.g. *of, by, for, before, as, without, about,* etc.

You can't risk taking out equipment that doesn't work.

I don't feel like working out.

As well as responding to emergencies …

We always start by checking the equipment.

Some verbs can be followed by an object + *-ing.*

We all have to spend an hour in the gym doing fitness work.

Examples of verbs followed by the *-ing* form

avoid

enjoy

feel like

finish

give up

involve

practise

risk

suggest

---

4 How many examples of verbs and prepositions followed by the *-ing* form can you find in the text?

Speaking

5 Complete these questions. Then ask and answer them with a partner. Give reasons for your answers.

1 Would you consider *working* as a firefighter? (*work*)
2 Would you enjoy _____ a job which involved danger? (*do*)
3 Would you do a job which involved _____ shifts? (*work*)
4 Would you do a job which meant _____ your social life? (*give up*)
5 Would you mind _____ to other countries for your job? (*travel*)
6 When you finish _____, do you want to get a job straightaway? (*study*)

What about becoming a ...?

- Who are the people you admire? What job do they do?

Reading

1 Read and complete the questions in the questionnaire.

> **What will you be doing in ten years' time?**
>
> **1** *What* sort of person are you? _____ three adjectives would you use to describe yourself?
> **2** _____ are you interested in?
> **3** _____ you an indoor person or an outdoor person?
> **4** _____ do you feel about taking risks?
> **5** _____ you think you will go to university?
> **6** _____ you good at working in a team?
> **7** _____ much time do you spend at the computer each day?
> **8** _____ you like to have your own business, or would you be happy to work for someone else?
> **9** _____ you consider working as a volunteer?
> **10** _____ are your ambitions?

Speaking

2 Work with a partner. Ask and answer the questions in Exercise 1.

3 Take turns to suggest a job for your partner based on his / her answers.

> What about becoming a (journalist / teacher)?
> What about working in (computing)?
> What about working for a (travel company)?

> That's not a bad idea.

> I don't think that would suit me, because ...

Writing

4 Write a paragraph about the job you'd like to do.

1 Describe yourself – what sort of person are you?
2 Say what you're good at.
3 Say what you're interested in.
4 Say what you hope you will be doing by the time you're 25.

I'm easy-going, patient and quite creative. I'm not an outdoor person. I'm good at working in a team. I'm interested in designing clothes and in making them, so I'd really like to work in fashion. By the time I'm 25, I hope I'll be working for a famous fashion designer.

Use of English: *will* future and future continuous

Use the *will* future for predictions of what you think or guess will happen.

Do you think you will go to university?

Use the future continuous to say that something will be in progress at a time in the future.

will + be + present participle

By the time I'm 25, I hope I'll be working for a famous fashion designer.

5 Use the prompts to write five sentences that are true for you. Start like this:

By the time I'm ..., I ...

By the time I'm 20, I'll be studying Law at university.

By the time I'm 30, I'll have a family.

- have a family
- drive a sports car
- live in another country
- work in ...
- study at university ...
- have a house/an apartment in ...

Project: A day in the life

6 Find out about a job that you'd like to do. Find out the answers to these questions. Use the Internet or other sources for your research.

1 What sort of person do you need to be?
2 Do you need a university degree to do this job?
3 What qualifications do you need?
4 What other skills do you need?
5 How long is the training?
6 Is the job well paid?
7 What are the good things about the job?
8 Are there any disadvantages?

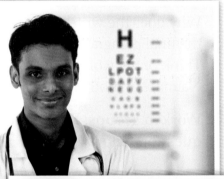

7 Give a presentation about the job to the class. The class can ask questions.

Fiction

1 Look at the picture. What is the girl doing? Where do you think she is?

2 Read the summary of the story so far and the extract on page 101. What is Naima's mother worried about and why?

3 Read the extract again and answer the questions.

1 Why is Naima glad that her sister is too far away to hear their parents' conversation? *(lines 5–6)*
2 Why does Naima's mother say, "If only *one* of our girls had been a boy!" *(lines 10–11)*?
3 How would you describe the father's attitude towards Naima and Rashida?
4 Is Rashida older or younger than Naima? How do you know?
5 Naima's mother says, "Alpanas can't put rice on the table". *(line 21)* What does she mean?
6 Why do you think Naima scrubs out her alpana design?
7 Why do you think Naima scowls before going into the hut?

4 Work with a partner. Discuss these questions.

1 Which words and phrases in the extract tell you about Naima's character?
2 Why does the writer use the adjectives 'plump', 'rich-looking' and 'juicy' in the final paragraph?
3 Think of the words you know to describe personality. Which ones describe Naima, her mother and father?

5 Work in groups. Read how the story continues and discuss the question below.

In order to help her family, Naima dresses as a boy so that she can drive the rickshaw while her father sleeps. However, she crashes the rickshaw, which means that the family is in even more trouble financially.

Naima learns of a rickshaw repair shop in a nearby town so she dresses up as a boy again and goes to the shop on the rickshaw. She's surprised to find that the person who owns the shop is a woman. She reveals that she is in fact a girl, and the woman hires her to paint alpanas on her rickshaws in return for doing repairs on Naima's father's rickshaw. The woman promises Naima that she can become an apprentice at the workshop in order to learn how to repair rickshaws herself.

When her father eventually finds Naima, he is angry at first but then is proud that his daughter has become so independent.

Did Naima do the right thing? Give your reasons.

The story so far

Naima is the central character of the story. She lives with her mother, father and sister Rashida. Their next-door neighbour is Saleem, who is the same age as Naima. Naima's father and Saleem's father are rickshaw drivers. Naima's father has just come home from work …

Rickshaw Girl

Mother's worried voice drifted through the open door: "How much did you earn this morning, Husband?"

Naima tried not to listen, but she couldn't help
5 it. She was glad Rashida was stooping over the marigolds in the back, too far away to hear.

"Not enough," Father replied.

Mother's sigh sounded like air leaking from a tyre. Naima counted to five. She braced herself for
10 words she'd overheard before. "If only *one* of our girls had been a boy!" Mother said.

Father gave his usual quick answer. "I have two wonderful daughters. They're just as good as boys."

"But you look so tired! Saleem takes his
15 father's rickshaw out every afternoon so his father can rest. Our girls can't do that for you."

"Isn't Naima the best *alpana* painter in the village?" Father asked. "Doesn't she take care of her sister like a tiger guarding a cub? And Rashida
20 is the best student in school!"

"Yes, but *alpanas* can't put rice on the table. And what use is it if Rashida is smart? We can't afford her school fees next year unless we pay off that rickshaw loan."

Rashida was coming back. Naima dunked the 25
rag in the half-empty pail of water her sister was carrying. Fiercely, she scrubbed out her *alpana* design until no traces of the rice powder remained on the threshold.

"What are you doing, Sister?" Rashida asked. 30
"You weren't finished! That was the best one yet!"

Naima didn't answer. Mother was right. All that a girl could do was cook, clean, wash clothes, and decorate; she wasn't allowed to do any work that brought in money. Painting *alpanas* wouldn't 35
help Father get rest. Or add to their earnings. It was a waste of time.

"Rash-ee-da! Na-ee-ma! Come inside! Your father is hungry."

Saleem drove by again. This time a plump 40
passenger sat on the bench of the rickshaw. He was a rich-looking passenger, juicy with money. Naima scowled and followed her sister into the hut.

Rickshaw Girl by Mitali Perkins; Charlesbridge Publishing, 2007

drifted *(line 1)* moved slowly as if carried by the wind

stooping *(line 5)* bending forward and down

marigolds *(line 6)* plants with bright yellow or orange flowers

sigh *(line 8)* a slow breath out which makes a long soft sound

leaking *(line 8)* coming out from a small hole

tyre *(line 9)* a thick rubber ring that fits around the wheel of a car, bicycle or other vehicle

braced herself *(line 9)* prepared herself for something unpleasant

overheard *(line 10)* heard what someone was saying to someone else, not to you

alpana *(line 17)* a pattern painted in the doorway of a house, using rice-powder paint

smart *(line 22)* clever

school fees *(line 23)* money you pay to go to school

loan *(line 24)* money you borrow

dunked *(line 25)* put something into a liquid and took it out again

pail *(line 26)* bucket

scrubbed out *(line 27)* rubbed out so that it disappeared

traces *(line 28)* a very small amount of something

threshold *(line 29)* the floor of an entrance

plump *(line 40)* quite fat

scowled *(line 43)* looked angrily

Review of Units 11–12

Vocabulary
Personality adjectives

1 **Read the descriptions and complete the adjectives.**

Someone who ...

1 likes exploring new places and doing new things is adv_____ .
2 avoids danger and doesn't take risks is cau_____ .
3 is good at making decisions quickly is dec_____ .
4 makes friends easily is soc_____ .
5 gives money or time to help people is gen_____ .
6 doesn't cheat or tell lies is hon_____ .
7 doesn't depend on other people for help and likes doing things in their own way is ind_____ .
8 doesn't like talking about themselves, their successes or their abilities is mod_____ .
9 has a negative view of the future is pess_____ .
10 gets angry very easily is qui_____-_____ .

Jobs

2 **Read the descriptions and write the job titles.**

1 A _____ looks after your teeth.
2 An _____ looks after your eyes and decides if you need glasses.
3 A _____ looks after your general health.
4 A _____ takes your order and brings your food in a restaurant.
5 A _____ repairs cars at a garage.
6 A _____ makes things from wood.
7 A _____ repairs water pipes.
8 A _____ works in a hotel or an office and greets people when they arrive.
9 A _____ puts out fires.
10 A _____ _____ teaches people to drive.

Use of English

3 **Complete the text using words from the two boxes.**

annoyed	aware	difficult
good	important	interested

at	for	in	of	to	with

I'm learning English, Spanish and Arabic. I'm _____ _____[1] going to other countries and perhaps working abroad one day. I'm quite _____ _____[2] learning new vocabulary and I've got a good memory. I'm _____ _____[3] the importance of languages in the modern world. At first, Arabic was _____ _____[4] me because I had to learn the alphabet, but it's fine now. Understanding the culture of other countries is very _____ _____[5] me. I get _____ _____[6] people who aren't interested in finding out about other parts of the world.

4 **Look at the adjectives and write the corresponding nouns.**

1 generous — *generosity*
2 modest
3 patient
4 arrogant
5 independent
6 kind
7 shy
8 optimistic
9 enthusiastic

5 Complete the sentences using the nouns suggested by the adjectives in brackets.

1 Iago in Shakespeare's play *Othello* called _____ 'the green-eyed monster'. (*jealous*)
2 _____ is an important aspect of friendship. (*loyal*)
3 Although he was sometimes afraid, he never showed his _____. (*afraid*)
4 It's good to have _____. It's good to aim high. (*ambitious*)
5 She showed great _____ by saying what she believed. (*brave*)
6 "_____ has driven the world crazy," said the American singer, Nina Simone. (*greedy*)

6 Complete the job titles with the correct suffixes.

-or	-ic	-ist	-ian	-er	-ant

1 journal____
2 manag____
3 pharmac____
4 electric____
5 design____
6 physiotherap____
7 taxi driv____
8 shop assist____
9 music____
10 swimming instruct____
11 paramed____
12 direct____
13 mechan____
14 police offic____
15 flight attend____
16 act____

7 Complete the sentences with a suitable verb in the *-ing* form.

1 I didn't feel like _____ to the concert, but I enjoyed it when I got there.
2 You can improve your balance by _____ on one leg.
3 It's best to avoid _____ before swimming.
4 Go over the footbridge. Don't risk _____ the road.
5 Our teachers have suggested _____ a day at the Science Museum.
6 Being a top tennis player involves _____ every day.
7 It's a good idea to spend time _____ the questions before you answer them.

8 She left without _____ a word.
9 Please switch off the lights before _____ the room.

8 Complete the conversation about a holiday. Use the future continuous (*will* + *be* + present participle, e.g. *we'll be flying*).

> Next week you're going on a special holiday. Here are the plans.
>
> | Monday 10.00 | flight to Athens |
> |---|---|
> | Tuesday | visit the Parthenon |
> | Wednesday | go on a trip to see the ancient theatre and stadium at Delphi |
> | Thursday | take a boat trip to three Greek islands, lunch on the boat |
> | Friday | shop for things to bring home |
> | Saturday | flight home |

A: *So tell me about this special holiday.*

B: *Well, on Monday morning we'll be flying [1] to Athens.*

A: *Wow! Will you be staying there all week?*

B: *Yes, we _____ [2] in Athens, but we _____ [3] quite a few trips.*

A: *So what _____ [4] on Tuesday?*

B: *We _____ [5] the Parthenon and then on Wednesday we _____ [6] to see the ancient theatre and stadium at Delphi.*

A: *Will you be flying there?*

B: *No, we _____ [7]. We _____ [8] by coach. And then on Thursday, we _____ [9] a boat trip to three islands and we _____ [10] lunch on the boat.*

A: *That sounds great. What happens on Friday?*

B: *I _____ [11] for things to bring home.*

A: *OK, make sure you bring me something!*

Shops and services

- **Topics** Supermarkets; the psychology of shopping; choosing a present and organising a celebration
- **Use of English** Prepositions followed by nouns; reflexive pronouns; prepositions after adjectives and verbs

In the aisles

- What are the advantages and disadvantages of supermarkets?

Vocabulary

1 Work with a partner. Identify the items in the photos.

> I think it's a carton of yoghurt. What do you think?

2 In which section of a supermarket would you find each item in Exercise 1?

- stationery -
- dairy products -
- bakery -
- household and cleaning -
- frozen foods -
- chilled foods -
- health and beauty -
- home baking -
- tinned foods -

3 Which other sections do you see in a supermarket?

Tea and coffee, ...

4 Write a list of two things you would find in each of the sections in Exercise 2.

<u>Dairy products</u>
butter, ...

5 Compare your lists. Did you all write down the same items?

> What did you put for dairy products?

Listening 25

6 Listen to these announcements. Which is the odd one out? Why?

7 Listen again. Which section of the supermarket does each announcement refer to?

Use of English: Prepositions followed by nouns

It's common to find prepositions before nouns in sales language.

preposition | noun

Today we have a special offer of three loaves of bread for the price of two.

---

8 Complete the details of the offers with the correct prepositions. Then listen and check.

> at   off (x 2)   on (x 3)   to   up

1 This week there's 20% _____ all dental products.
2 Did you know that this week you can get _____ _____ 20% _____ all your household and cleaning items if you have a store card?
3 We have delicious frozen desserts _____ offer this week, _____ half price.
4 We have ten different varieties _____ display.
5 Don't forget that ice cubes are now _____ sale.

Writing

9 Write a paragraph about the advantages and disadvantages of supermarkets.

The psychology of shopping

- What do supermarkets have in common?

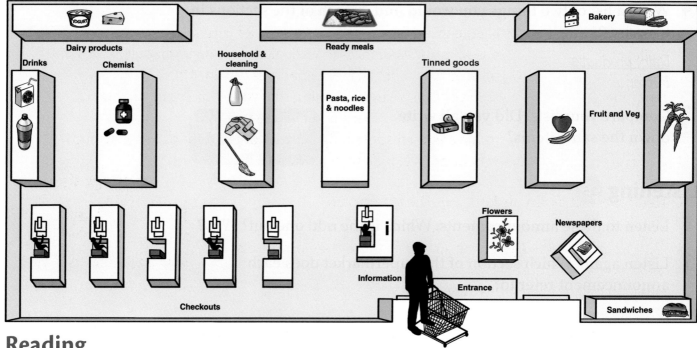

Reading

1 Read the text and look at the diagram. Which sections on the diagram does the article mention?

We have ways of making you buy

You arrive at the supermarket and what do you see? Flowers, newspapers and sandwiches for people in a hurry, on their way to work, on their way home, on their way to see a friend, ... The entrance area is arranged to look like a small shop. It's easy to find what you need. You help yourself to what you want, you pay and you're off. This store makes shopping easy, so why not go back when you do your weekly shopping?

Next, you come to the fruit and vegetable section. But why is it here and not at the end, near the checkout? The fruit and vegetables will get squashed if you put them at the bottom of your basket or your trolley. However, they give a wonderful impression of freshness and health. You can even select the items you want and weigh them yourself. It makes you feel you're getting the best possible quality.

You need the essentials: bread, rice and noodles. 'But where are they?' you ask yourself. You can smell the bread. Mmm, delicious! You head towards the lovely smell of freshly-baked bread which is on display at the back of the store. How can you resist?

Where's the bottled water? It's not next to the bakery. To get there, you have to pass the ready meals section with the most tempting goods at eye level. You pick up things you didn't know you needed.

Finally, you get to the checkout with far more in your trolley than you had on your shopping list. While you're waiting to pay, you see shelves full of little bars of chocolate. Just what you need after all that shopping. Go on, why not treat yourself? You deserve it!

Vocabulary

2 Match the words to the definitions.

1	checkout	a	important things that you need
2	squashed	b	a large metal basket on wheels used for carrying shopping
3	trolley	c	passages for customers to walk along in a supermarket
4	essentials	d	pressed into a flat shape, sometimes causing damage
5	tempting	e	stop yourself doing something that you want to do
6	resist	f	the place in the supermarket where you pay
7	aisles	g	to have earned something because of good (or bad) behaviour
8	deserve	h	very attractive, making you want it

3 Read the text again and answer the questions.

1 Why is the title 'We have ways of making you buy'?
2 Give examples from the text of some of the ways supermarkets make you spend money.
3 Which of the following describes the text? Give reasons for your choice.
   a It's written by a supermarket manager, to help you find your way around the store.
   b It's an advertising feature, promoting a supermarket.
   c It's a magazine feature, giving the writer's opinion of supermarkets.

4 Complete the sentences with the correct reflexive pronouns.

1 You can help *yourself* to a free sample of cheese at our dairy counter.
2 I'm going to make _____ a nice stir fry with these fresh noodles.
3 Can you pack your things _____? Or do you need any help?
4 Stop playing with that trolley! You'll hurt _____.
5 We always treat _____ to a nice dessert at the weekend.
6 Most customers like to choose their fruit and vegetables _____.

> **Language tip**
>
> | Singular | Plural |
> |---|---|
> | shelf | shelves |
>
> *aisle* is pronounced like *I'll*

> **Use of English: Reflexive pronouns**
>
> *myself, yourself, himself, herself, itself ourselves, yourselves, themselves*
>
> We use reflexive pronouns with verbs when the object is the same person (or thing) as the subject.
>
> *You help yourself to what you want.*
>
> We also use reflexive pronouns to emphasise the subject or object.
>
> *You can even weigh them yourself.*

Speaking

5 Work in groups. Talk about your local supermarket.

1 Does your supermarket follow the pattern of the typical supermarket described in the article?
2 Does it often have special offers? Give examples.
3 How does it make you want to buy things?

The best present

- What do you need to think about when you're choosing a present for a friend?

Listening 26

1 Listen to Lara and Julia. What are they planning?

2 Listen again and answer the questions.

1 What are the girls going to get from the supermarket?
2 What are they going to ask Mrs Da Silva about?
3 Lara talks about 'having a collection'. What does this mean and why are they going to have one?
4 What are they going to buy Emiko? What's the reason for their choice?
5 Where are they going to buy the presents?

3 Complete the sentences with the correct prepositions: *as, for, from, on, to, with.* Then listen again to check.

1 We can get those *from* the supermarket.
2 How we're going to pay ___ it all?
3 Emiko is really keen ___ tennis.
4 She belongs ___ a tennis club.
5 I was thinking ___ something to do with tennis.
6 She'll be really pleased ___ that.

4 Which of these does Lara do to explain the word *sun visor*?

She describes ...
- where you wear it.
- what shape it is.
- what it looks like.
- where you buy it.
- what it's used for.
- what it's made of.

Use of English: Prepositions after adjectives and verbs

Adjectives and verbs are sometimes followed by prepositions. Try to learn them as whole phrases.

Adjective + preposition
Be nice to your little brother!
Are you afraid of spiders?

Verb + preposition
I'm looking for a present for my friend.
I agree with you.

Language tip

Lara couldn't remember the word *sun visor.* Notice how she explained what she meant:

Lara: What about one of those things, you know, you wear it on your head?

Julia: You mean a baseball cap?

Lara: No, it hasn't got a top, but it protects your eyes from the sun. You know what I mean.

Julia: A sun visor?

Lara: Yes, that's it.

Speaking

5 Work with a partner. Take turns to describe the things in the pictures without saying their names. Use *you know* and *you know what I mean.*

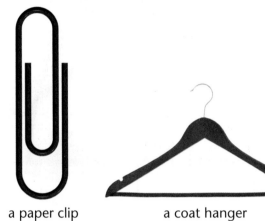

a paper clip   a coat hanger   a button   an envelope

6 Think of three more objects. Describe them to your partner without saying their names. Your partner has to guess what you're talking about.

Project: Plan a celebration

7 Work in groups. One of your friends is leaving the school. You're going to have a surprise celebration and buy a present for him / her.

- First discuss what you need for the celebration (food, drinks, music, etc.) and decide on a present. Use the language from the dialogue in Exercise 1 in your discussion. Listen again if necessary.

1 Write a list of the jobs that need to be done and who's going to do them.

Action plan		
Job	Who?	Where?
make sandwiches, etc.	everybody	at home
buy a cake	Tanya	Lina's Pâtisserie

2 Present your action plan to the class.
3 The class can interrupt with questions.

> We're going to make some food for the celebration and we're going to buy a cake from Lina's Pâtisserie.

> What sort of cake are you going to get?

Possessions and personal space

- **Topics** Treasured possessions; my room; buying and selling
- **Use of English** *to have something done*; past perfect in reported speech; compound adjectives

Treasured possessions

- What are your most treasured possessions?

Reading

1 Read the posts on the web forum. What are the items pictured here?

What are your most treasured possessions?

Emma, 13

I have an old teddy bear which my mum gave me when I was a baby. It was hers when she was younger. His ear came off, but Mum had it repaired.
I love him to bits, but I let my baby sister play with him when she wants to!

Leelah, 14

I've kept my Olympics tickets. Going to the Olympics was the best day of my life. My dad had the tickets framed and I've got them on the wall in my room.

Jodie, 12

All my sports trophies are special to me. I keep them in a glass cabinet in my room.

Cara, 12

I was a bridesmaid for my cousin when I was six. I've still got the dress, the tiara and the bouquet.

Marta, 13

One of my most prized possessions is my flute. I saved up for it for two years so I always put it away in its case and I look after it.

Eric, 15

My most treasured possessions are my family, my computer and the Real Madrid football shirt that my dad had signed for me by Xabi Alonso.

Natasha, 14

I treasure the friendship bracelet that my friend made for me before she moved house.

Lee, 13

My most treasured possession is my primary school class photo. I had it signed by everyone on my last day. It reminds me of all my friends!

2 Answer the questions.

1 Emma says *I love him to bits* when she's talking about her teddy bear. What do you think this means?
2 Who takes part in competitive events?
3 Who plays a musical instrument?
4 Who has the name of a famous person on one of their prized possessions?
5 For whom is friendship important?

Language tip

These phrasal verbs may be useful when you're talking about personal possessions:

come off   save up

look after   put away

Speaking

3 Work in groups. Read the posts on the web forum again. Which of the posts give you an idea of what the person is like? You can use the adjectives in the box.

determined	easy-going	independent	kind	loyal
organised	sociable	competitive	enthusiastic	

4 Give advice using the verbs in the box.

clean	deliver	frame	repair

1 – I'd like to <u>put these photos up</u> on the wall of my room.
  – You should *have them framed*.
2 – I've got a gold watch that my grandfather gave me, but it's broken.
  – You should _____.
3 – I've got a lovely silk jacket that belonged to my great-grandmother, but it's dirty and you can't wash it.
  – You should _____.
4 – I'd like to send my friend some chocolates, but they'll get squashed in the post.
  – You should _____.

Use of English: *to have something done*

If you have something done, someone does it for you. You don't do it yourself.

have + object + past participle

Mum had it repaired. (= Mum didn't repair the teddy bear herself. She asked someone else to do it.)
The past participle has a passive meaning so you can say who did the action using *by*.
My dad had it signed by Xabi Alonso.

Speaking and writing

5 Work with a partner. Talk about your most treasured possessions. Then write your own post for the web forum.

My space

- Look at the picture. Do you think it shows a boy's room or a girl's room?

  How many of the things in the picture can you name?

Vocabulary

1 Look at the list. Which of the things can you see in the picture?

- drawers
- bunk beds
- cupboard
- reading lamp
- cushion
- hook

- chair
- snowboard
- storage basket
- trunk
- baseball cap
- goggles

- guitar
- book
- noticeboard
- ladder
- stool
- mirror

Listening 🔘27

2 Look at the picture of Yann's room on page 112. Listen and point to the things as they are mentioned.

3 Listen to the interview again. From what he says, what do we learn about Yann, his interests and his personality?

Use of English: Past perfect in reported speech

When we tell people what someone said, we usually change the tense, because what they said was in the past.

Direct speech	Reported speech
Present perfect	**Past perfect**
"I've only had it for a few months."	*He said he had only had it for a few months.*
Past simple	**Past perfect**
"I saved up for it for quite a long time."	*He said he had saved up for it for quite a long time.*

---

4 Report the answers to the interviewer's questions.

1 "Is that your snowboard? It looks new. How long have you had it?"
Yann said he had only had it for a few months.

2 "What about the animal's head?"
He said ...

3 "What are you reading at the moment?"
He said ...

4 "Is your room always this tidy?"
He said ...

Speaking

5 Work with a partner. Take turns to describe something in the picture without giving its name. Your partner has to guess what it is.

A *It's made of metal. You can put things in it or on it.*

B *Is it a trunk?*

A *Yes, it is.*

6 Work in groups. Talk about Yann's room. What do you like about it? What don't you like about it?

For sale

Reading

1 Read the adverts on the school noticeboard. Which is the odd one out? Why?

For sale
Junior tennis racket, hardly used. Well-known make. Complete with cover.

For sale
Multi-sport helmet in good condition. Suitable for skateboarding, cycling, roller skating.
Colour: pink. Reason for sale: owner outgrown.

To give away
A book of bedtime stories. Classic stories from all over the world. Would suit a younger brother or sister!

Wanted
Kind, patient animal lover wanted to look after my well-behaved cat for two weeks while I'm on holiday.

For sale
Multi-coloured baseball boots. In original box, never worn. Reason for sale: too small.

2 Which extra piece of information goes with each advert?

- Kneepads, wrist guards and elbow pads also available.
- Would suit young player.
- Size 35; white laces
- Beautiful pictures and in very good condition.
- Food and own bed provided.

Use of English: Compound adjectives

You can use two words together to make a compound adjective.

well-known *It's a well-known make of tennis racket.*
  JK Rowling is a well-known author.

---

3 Look at these compound adjectives from the adverts. What do they mean?

1 hardly used *It has hardly ever been used. / It has almost never been used.*
2 well-known
3 multi-sport
4 well-behaved
5 multi-coloured

> **Language tip**
>
> In short advertisements, we often write in note form rather than in full sentences.

Writing

4 Write out each advertisement in Exercise 1 using full sentences.

1 *This junior tennis racket has hardly ever been used. It is a well-known make. It comes complete with a cover. It would suit a young player.*

Project: Organise a charity sale

5 Work in two big groups, A and B. Each group should do the following:

1 Write a list of all the items that you will bring to the charity sale.
- Think of things that you hardly ever use and want to give away.
- Think of things that you can make.
2 Write the catalogue of items for sale.
- Write the adverts for each item.
- Create a small booklet containing the adverts. Use small photos or drawings if you can.
3 Make a poster showing the date and the time and place of the sale.

Autobiography

Floella Benjamin is an actress, author, television presenter, singer, business woman and politician.

1 What do you know about Trinidad?

2 Read this extract from Chapter 1 of Floella Benjamin's autobiography *Coming to England*. She is describing the family home in Trinidad, in the Caribbean. Do you think she enjoyed living there?

Coming to England

Life in Trinidad

The house we lived in was a small wooden building on stilts with dazzling whitewashed walls. There were windows and doors at the front and the back. We had two bedrooms which were the scene of many pillow fights
5 and trampolining sessions, a small washroom with a sink and cold tap, an airy kitchen with a large glassless louvred window where we also ate all our meals, and finally a sitting room where no one was allowed except on special occasions or when we had visitors.
10   This room was my mother's pride and joy. Its brilliant white curtains always smelt fresh and the mahogany furniture was always highly polished, as was the wooden floor. My sister and I spent many hours polishing and shining that room from as far back as I can remember.
15 We had to do the polishing before we left for school each day. The comfortable wooden chairs in the room were draped with crisp white lace headrests and the round table, which we ate from on Sundays and other special occasions, had a doily in its centre, on which sat a vase
20 of glorious fresh flowers. These were from our small front garden which was full of exotic, sweet-smelling flowers and shrubs such as beautiful flame-red hibiscus which seemed to attract swarms of exquisite butterflies and hovering hummingbirds, in search of nectar. The backyard
25 was where Marmie grew vegetables for our kitchen, like pigeon peas, cassavas, okras and dasheen. A tall bushy tree stood in the yard, reaching up to the kitchen window, and whenever one of us had a bad cold, Marmie would pick some of the leaves, boil them and give us the vile-
30 tasting liquid to drink. It always made us better – I guess the thought of a second dose was enough to do the trick! Also in the backyard was a galvanised shower unit where

we had our baths. There was no hot tap but the cold water was always warm because of the heat of the sun. During
35 the drought season, from around January to May, we would have to get water from a standpipe in the street. Everyone would queue up with large enamel buckets, oil cans, basins – anything big enough to carry the water.
    The washing was done under the house in a big
40 wooden tub with a scrubbing board, and the washing lines hung between two trees in the backyard. Our car was also parked under the house.

by Floella Benjamin

stilts *(line 2)* posts that a house is built on to raise it above the ground

whitewashed *(line 2)* painted white

pillow *(line 4)* a cushion for resting your head on in bed

glassless *(line 6)* without glass

louvred *(line 6)* with flat sloping pieces of wood, metal, or glass across it to allow light and air to come in while keeping rain out

mahogany *(line 11)* a dark reddish-brown wood used for furniture

polished *(line 12)* made to shine by rubbing it

draped *(line 17)* put across so that it hangs loosely

lace *(line 17)* a decorative cloth made by twisting thread into patterns

doily *(line 19)* a piece of paper or cloth with a pattern in it used as a decoration on a plate or table

exotic *(line 21)* unusual or interesting because it comes from a foreign country

shrub *(line 22)* a bush, particularly one that is planted in the garden

hibiscus *(line 22)* a tropical plant or bush with large brightly coloured flowers

swarms *(line 23)* large groups of insects flying together

hovering *(line 24)* staying up in the air without moving anywhere

hummingbird *(line 24)* a very small brightly coloured bird with a long thin beak

nectar *(line 24)* a sweet liquid that bees, other insects and some birds collect from flowers

dose *(line 31)* a measured amount of medicine

standpipe *(line 36)* a vertical pipe which connects the water supply to a public place

scrubbing board *(line 40)* a wooden board used for washing clothes

3 The author uses the following 'strong' adjectives. Match them with their meanings.

1 dazzling *(line 2)*
2 brilliant *(line 10)*
3 glorious *(line 20)*
4 exquisite *(line 23)*
5 vile *(line 29)*

a very bad
b very bright (x 2)
c very beautiful, making you feel very happy
d very delicate, very fine

Language tip

Strong adjectives have the idea of 'very' in them so you don't use *very* before them.

4 The author uses compound adjectives and two or more adjectives together to intensify the descriptions. Look at the examples and find five more in the text.

brilliant white curtains, comfortable wooden chairs

5 Read the extract again. Then answer the questions.

1 What impression do you get of the climate in Trinidad?
2 What impression do you get of Floella's mother, 'Marmie'?
3 What do you learn about the family's household chores and everyday life?
4 What do the details about plants and nature tell you about the place?

6 Work in groups. You're going to imagine and then describe a house.

- Take 30 seconds to imagine a very beautiful house – the sort of house you would like to live in.
- When you have a clear picture of the house in your mind, take it in turns to describe it to the other members of the group.
- You can use words and phrases from the extract.
- The other members of the group either draw the house you describe or write notes about it. They can ask you questions as you're talking.
- When you've finished, check to see if the other students understood your description.

Review of Units 13–14

Vocabulary

Supermarkets and shopping

1 Match the words in the two columns to describe six sections of a supermarket.

1 chilled
2 dairy
3 health and
4 household and
5 home
6 ready

a baking
b beauty
c cleaning
d foods
e meals
f products

2 Answer the questions using the words from the box.

| bakery | checkout | dairy products |
| frozen foods | stationery | tinned foods |

To which aisle or part of the supermarket do you go if you want to

1 buy a notepad and a pen?
2 buy a loaf of bread?
3 buy a carton of yoghurt and some cheese?
4 buy a tin of tomatoes?
5 buy a carton of ice cream?
6 pay for your shopping?

Use of English

3 Choose the correct word.

1 Get three packets of biscuits *for / on* the price of two.
2 This week there is 10% *from / off* all cleaning products.
3 All ready meals are *at / on* offer this week.
4 Buy two large cartons of yoghurt and get the second *on / at* half price.
5 Barbecues will be *on / in* sale next week. Place your order now!
6 Order online and get *up to / down from* 10% off your normal shopping bill.

4 Complete the sentences with the correct reflexive pronouns, e.g. *myself, yourself,* etc.

1 My brother's just bought <u>himself</u> a guitar.
2 I painted my room _____. Do you like it?
3 There's some milk in the fridge. Make _____ a milkshake.
4 My best friend gave me this bracelet. She made it _____.
5 Listen, you two. Be careful when you're lifting that heavy trunk. You might hurt _____.
6 My grandparents treated _____ to a new TV.
7 I hope you don't mind, but we helped _____ to some of that nice cake that's in the kitchen.
8 The radio on my alarm clock switches _____ off after an hour.

5 Rewrite the questions and sentences to give the same meaning, using the adjectives in brackets.

1 Do you like your new ski boots?
 Are you pleased with your new ski boots?
 (*pleased*)
2 Don't get angry with your little brother.
 (*nice*)
3 My friend has a fear of spiders.
 (*afraid*)
4 I like photography.
 (*keen*)
5 You always get top marks in Maths.
 (*good*)

6 Complete the sentences with the correct prepositions.

1 Are you looking _____ your keys? They're on the hook behind the door.
2 Yes, you're right. I agree _____ you.
3 Could you get something _____ the supermarket for me?
4 Make sure you've got enough money to pay _____ the shopping.
5 Does this watch belong _____ you?
6 What colour are you thinking _____ painting this room?

7 Read the signs and write what you can have done at each place.

> PROFESSIONAL CLEANERS
> All types of clothes

1 You can have your clothes cleaned here.

> We repair shoes while you wait

2 _____

> Monday–Friday
> Car wash free when you buy
> 50 litres of fuel

3 _____

> Come in for a haircut.
> No appointment necessary

4 _____

> We take your photo in a studio setting

5 _____

8 Report these statements. Remember to use the past perfect.

1 "I've found some family photos at the bottom of a drawer."
He said *he had found some family photos at the bottom of the drawer*.

2 "I've bought a flute with my pocket money."
She said _____.

3 "I made a cake at the weekend."
He said _____.

4 "I saw a really good film on TV."
She said _____.

5 "I haven't had time to practise the guitar."
He said _____.

6 "I didn't do very well in the exam."
She said _____.

15 Natural disasters

- **Topics** Natural disasters; raising money for charity
- **Use of English** Present perfect active and passive; *despite, in spite of*; modals

Dangerous nature

- Which natural disasters have been in the news recently?

Reading

1 Read these definitions. They will help you understand the text in Exercise 2.

1	pressure	the force pressing on something
2	release	allow to escape
3	vibrations	fast and continuous shaking movements
4	surface	the outside or top layer of something
5	fuel	a substance that produces heat or power when it is burned
6	source	the origin or provider of something
7	overflow	(of a liquid) not able to be contained
8	melt	change from a solid into liquid
9	burst	break suddenly so that the contents come out
10	epicentre	the area of land directly over the centre of an earthquake

2 Read the text. Choose a title for each paragraph.

- Earthquakes
- Floods
- Hurricanes
- Wildfires

Earth, wind, fire and water

① These start over the warm ocean waters near the equator. Warm moist air rises and then cools to form clouds. Cooler air moves in to replace the warm air and it too becomes warm and rises.

② The earth's crust – its outer layer – is made up of moving plates. Sometimes these plates press against each other and the pressure is so great that it has to be released. When this happens, vibrations travel up to the earth's surface.

③ They can move at speeds of over 20 kilometres an hour, burning everything in their path: trees, homes, animals and of course people. They happen when the following three things come together: fuel, oxygen and a heat source. This is called 'the fire triangle'.

④ These occur when there is very heavy rain, causing rivers to overflow their banks. They can also be caused by ice melting very quickly or by a dam bursting, allowing a lot of water to escape.

3 Choose an illustration for each paragraph of the text.

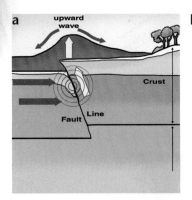
a

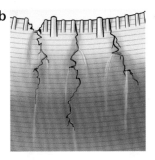
b

c

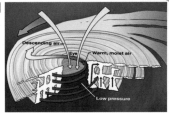
d

4 Find the final sentence for each paragraph in Exercise 2.

a The heat source can be lightning, a campfire, a match and even the sun.

b The energy is released in waves which are felt most strongly at the epicentre.

c This creates a circular movement of clouds and wind which becomes faster and faster, producing a massive storm.

d Bridges, houses, trees and cars can be picked up and carried away.

Listening 28

5 Listen to the news report. What kind of natural disaster does it describe? Can you tell from the rescue workers' accent where the disaster has happened?

6 Complete the sentences with the correct present perfect form of the verbs in brackets.

1 They _____ here for food, water and, if they're lucky, some clean clothes. (*come*)

2 I _____ to two volunteer firefighters. (*speak*)

3 I _____ anything like this in my life. (*never / see*)

4 Two hundred people _____. (*kill*)

5 Remote villages _____ the worst. (*hit*)

> ### Use of English: Present perfect, active and passive
>
> We often use the present perfect for reporting news, when a particular past time is not specified.
>
> **Active**
>
> *They've lost their homes.*
>
> **Passive**
>
> *Thousands of homes have been destroyed.*

Discussion

7 Work in groups. Which of the natural disasters on these pages do you think is the most frightening and why?

Drought in East Africa

- Why is water important for life?

Reading

1 Read this report by ActionAid. Why do you think it was written?

Sabria, 15, from Kenya, is looking after her niece. Her mother, Zeinabu, has lost her animals because there is no water. She can no longer afford to pay for Sabria to go to school.

A severe drought across some East African countries (Kenya, Ethiopia, Somalia, Uganda and Djibouti) has left at least ten million people in urgent need of help. It is the worst drought in over 60 years. Crops have failed and many animals have died, leaving people with no food. The United Nations says that 250,000 children are seriously malnourished.

In Kenya, the charity ActionAid is working hard to give emergency help to people. However, in spite of the charity's efforts, five million people are in urgent need of food and the situation is likely to get worse over the next few months. Some families are only eating one meal a day and children are missing school in order to help their families.

Sabria, her sister and her sister's children live with her mother, Zeinabu , in a small room in another family's house. Zeinabu used to have 180 cows and 200 goats. However, they have all died because of the drought. Zeinabu says:"We live on the food the charity gives us: maize, beans, porridge and cooking oil. What we get for a month would normally only be enough for a week."

Sabria, 15, from Kenya, looking after her niece in drought stricken Africa

"We go to bed hungry every night. I sing for the small ones when they are crying, but they always end up crying themselves to sleep. Water has become a problem. We don't wash any more. We drink all the water we get, and it is still not enough."

Despite such extreme circumstances, Zeinabu and Sabria are both hopeful for the future. Sabria is hoping to go back to school and wants to become a police officer when she is older.

(Adapted from *East Africa drought and food crisis, 2011*)

PHOTO: Søren Bjerregard Jepsen/MS ActionAid Denmark

Vocabulary

2 Work with a partner. Find these words in the report and work out their meaning from the context. If you're unsure, use a dictionary.

1 severe
2 drought
3 urgent
4 malnourished
5 circumstances

Reading

3 **Read the report again and answer the questions.**

1 What is the crisis described in the report and who has it affected?
2 How has the crisis affected Sabria and her family?
3 How are people surviving?
4 Is the situation going to improve in the near future?
5 How does the report end and why do you think it ends in this way?

4 **Rewrite the sentences using the structures in brackets.**

1 Although they were hungry, the children managed to sleep. (*despite* + -*ing* form)
   Despite being hungry, the children managed to sleep.
2 Although there is a severe drought, Sabria and her family have some water to drink. (*in spite of* + noun phrase)
3 Although she doesn't go to school at the moment, Sabria hopes to return in the future. (*despite* + -*ing* form)
4 Although they have these problems, they remain positive. (*in spite of* + pronoun)
5 Although they work hard to look after their animals, there's nothing people can do when there is no rain. (*despite* + -*ing* form)

> ## Use of English: *despite, in spite of*
>
> *Despite* and *in spite of* have the same meaning.
>
> Like *although*, *despite* and *in spite of* introduce a contrast.
>
> *In spite of / Despite the charity's efforts, five million people are in urgent need of food.*
>
> After *despite* or *in spite of*, we use a noun (or noun phrase), a pronoun or the -*ing* form of the verb.
>
> `noun phrase`
> *Despite such extreme circumstances, Zeinabu and Sabria are both hopeful for the future.*
>
> `pronoun`
> *Despite this, they have continued to have a positive attitude.*
>
> `-ing form`
> *Despite having very little food and water, they are managing to survive.*

Speaking

5 Work in groups. Discuss the problems that are caused by drought. Look back at the ActionAid report to help you. You may also include these ideas:

| dehydration | famine (serious lack of food) | malnourishment | disease |

Writing

6 Write a short information leaflet for ActionAid, telling people about the drought in East Africa or about another serious situation. You don't need to use full sentences – you can use note form. Use no more than 50 words.

● *10 million people affected in 5 countries*

Raising money for charity

- When and why do people raise money for charity?

Reading

1 Charity fêtes are often held in villages in Britain during the summer. Read about games to play at a charity fête. Choose one of them and draw a picture to illustrate it.

One of the ways to raise money for charity is to have a school fête. Here are some ideas for games you can play at the fête. People pay to play each game.

A coconut shy

Put some posts in the ground. Put a coconut on the top of each post. Give people three wooden balls or cricket balls to throw at the coconuts. To win a prize, you need to knock a coconut off a post.

Apple bobbing

Fill a large bowl or bucket with water. Put some apples in the water. The apples will float. People try to pick up an apple with their teeth. You can only use your teeth. You mustn't use your hands.

Beans in the jar

Fill a large jar with dried beans. Count them as you put them in. (Write the number down somewhere.) People have to guess how many beans there are in the jar. Write their name down and the number they guessed. At the end of the fête, the person who has made the best guess wins a prize. You don't have to get the exact number, just the nearest.

Pin the tail on the donkey

A picture of a donkey with a missing tail is put on the wall or a noticeboard. To play the game, you must be blindfolded (your eyes are covered so that you can't see). You are turned round several times so that you don't know which way you're facing. Then you are given the donkey's tail and you have to pin it on the donkey in the correct place. You can only use one hand.

Sack race

Each competitor stands in a sack. They have to jump in the sack from the starting line to the finishing line. The first person to cross the finishing line is the winner.

2 Work with a partner. Take turns to explain the games to your partner without looking at the text. Remember to use the correct modal verbs (look at the *Use of English* box on page 125). Your partner can correct you and ask questions about any details that you forget.

Listening 29

3 Listen to a conversation. What event is about to take place?

4 Listen again and answer the questions.

1 What does Steve ask Mrs Oakman about?
2 Describe Mrs Oakman's attitude to Steve.
3 Why does Mrs Oakman say the event is going to be a disaster?
4 What happened two years ago?
5 Why can bad weather be an advantage for an event like this?
6 How would you describe Mrs Oakman's attitude to Major Fortescue?
7 What is the difference between Mrs Oakman's opinion at the beginning of the conversation and at the end?

Project: A charity fête

5 Work in groups. Organise a school fête for charity.

1 Plan the event.
  ● Decide on a charity.
  ● Decide on a date, time and place.
  ● Decide how you're going to advertise it, e.g. posters, leaflets, letters, etc.
  ● Decide on the games and activities you're going to have.
2 Draft a letter to parents. Explain what you're doing and why.
3 Ask your teacher to check your letter. Then do a final version.

> **Use of English: Modals**
>
> Use *can / can't* to express:
>
> ● possibility and ability
>
> *Here are some ideas for games you can play.*
> *Your eyes are covered so that you can't see.*
>
> ● permission
> *You can only use your teeth.*
> *You can only use one hand.*
>
> Use *must* and *have to* for rules.
> *You must be blindfolded.*
> *People have to guess how many beans there are in the jar.*
>
> Use *mustn't* for negative orders (= don't do this).
> *You mustn't use your hands.*
>
> Use *don't have to* to say that something is not necessary.
> *You don't have to get the exact number.*

(*School address*)
(*Date*)

Dear Parents

On 20th June from 2 to 5 in the afternoon, we're going to have a fête in the courtyard.

We're raising money for ... We're doing this because ...

We plan to have several games and activities. For example, ...

We hope to see you at the fête.

Yours sincerely,

Class 8

---

4 Design a poster for the fête.

- **Topics** Disasters and survival; survival kits
- **Use of English** Comparative adverbs

Amazing survival

- Can you remember any news stories in which people have survived disasters?

Reading

1 Read this extract from a book review. What is remarkable about Juliane Koepcke's story?

Juliane Koepcke was 17 when she was flying with her mother to Lima in Peru. Lightning struck the plane and there was an explosion. Suddenly, she was falling through the air, still strapped to her seat, 3,000 metres above the Peruvian rainforest. She lost consciousness and when she came round, she was still strapped into her seat. She had cuts and bruises on her arms and legs and she had broken her collarbone, but that was all. She was the only survivor out of the 92 people on board. "I was too shocked to feel frightened," she says. "When I heard the sound of running water, I knew I had to follow it, because a river would lead to human settlement." Her survival instinct took over. She drank dirty water and walked for ten days in the rainforest before she was found. "The accident changed me completely," she says. "I have learned that life is precious – that it can be taken from you at any moment. I came so close to death then that everyday stress no longer affects me. Trivial things don't worry me any more."

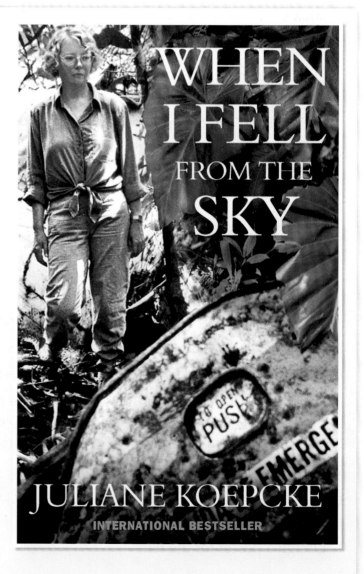

WHEN I FELL FROM THE SKY

JULIANE KOEPCKE

INTERNATIONAL BESTSELLER

Vocabulary

2 Find these words and phrases in the review. Try to work out their meaning from the context. If you're unsure, use a dictionary.

1 an explosion
2 strapped to her seat
3 she lost consciousness
4 she came round
5 cuts and bruises
6 collarbone
7 survivor
8 survival instinct
9 precious
10 trivial

3 Read the review again and answer the questions.

1 What was the plane's destination?
2 Why did the plane come down?
3 How high was the plane flying?
4 How many people were travelling on the plane?
5 Where did Juliane land?
6 How long was she there?

Listening 30

4 Listen to this extract from a radio programme. What are the similarities with Juliane's story?

5 Listen again and complete the details below.

Writing

6 Use the information in Exercise 5 to write a paragraph about Bahia, similar to the paragraph about Juliane.

Name	Bahia Bakari
Age at the time of the accident	_____
Destination	Comoros Islands, off the ____ coast of Africa
Where did the plane crash?	_____
Number of passengers on board	_____
Number of survivors	_____
Injuries	broken ____ and burns
How long was it before she was rescued?	_____

Speaking

7 Work in groups. Discuss these questions.

1 In your opinion, what are the most surprising aspects of these stories?
2 What are the positive aspects of the stories?

Surviving together

- What is mining? What materials do people mine for?

Reading

1 Read the article. Who were 'the 33' and why did they become famous?

The 33

1   On 5th August 2010, part of a gold and copper mine in northern Chile collapsed. Thirty-three miners were trapped 700 metres below ground. They tried to escape through the mine's ventilation system, but they couldn't. One of the miners, Luis Urzúa, persuaded the others that they should stay together as a group.

2   There were emergency supplies of food and water in the shelter, but only enough for two or three days. The men had to make them last much longer. They decided that they should work as a team and take decisions by majority vote. Everything was voted on; this included how to share the food and what jobs each person should do. It was important to use the strengths of each individual in order to keep their spirits up, to avoid conflict and to survive.

3   Meanwhile, rescuers were carefully drilling down into the rock to see if they could find any signs of life. For several days the trapped miners heard the drills getting closer. On 22nd August, a drill broke through into the space where the miners were. The miners attached a note to it. It said 'Estamos bien en el refugio' (= We're OK in the shelter). Next, video cameras were sent down  the drill hole and pictures of the men were seen by their families and the rescuers.

4   After the drill broke through, the rescuers were able to send down food and water in blue plastic capsules to the trapped miners. A month later, the men were still there, as teams of rescuers attempted to drill shafts deep and wide enough to bring them out.

   A team of engineers from the Chilean navy designed a special steel capsule, just wider than a man's shoulders, to bring the miners up through the narrow shaft to the surface. On 12th October, the rescue began. The capsule brought up the men one by one. The operation worked better and it was completed more quickly than the rescuers had originally estimated.

5

2 Read these sentences. Which paragraph in the article does each sentence complete?

a In less than 24 hours, all the men had been brought to safety.

b As a group, they would be much more likely to survive.

c The older miners, for example, helped to give 19-year-old Jimmy Sánchez the confidence that they would be rescued.

d The rescue operation was reported much more widely than previous mining rescue attempts because the video footage was shown on TV news broadcasts around the world.

e By 24th September, the miners had been trapped underground for 50 days, longer than anyone else in history.

3 Write eight questions about the story using these question words.

1 Where and when
2 How many
3 How far
4 How much
5 How
6 When
7 What
8 On what date

4 Work with a partner. Take turns to ask and answer the questions you wrote in Exercise 3.

5 Complete the sentences using the prompts.

1 My handwriting is terrible. You write _much more clearly_ than I do. (much, clear)

2 You'd be able to see the board _____ if you sat in the front row. (much, easy)

3 We can get home _____ if we take the bus. (much, quick)

4 I work _____ when I listen to music. (much, good)

5 They played _____ than usual because they hadn't trained enough. (much, bad)

Speaking

6 Work in groups. Discuss this question.

What lessons can be learned from this story?

Use of English: Comparative adverbs

To make comparative adverbs, use *more* + adverb (*than*).

The operation was completed more quickly than the rescuers had originally estimated.

Some comparative adverbs are irregular:

Adverb	Comparative adverb
well	better
badly	worse

The operation worked better than the rescuers had originally estimated.

To make comparisons stronger, use *much* + *more* + adverb (*than*).

The rescue operation was reported much more widely than previous mining rescue attempts.

Survival kit

- When and why would you need a survival kit?

1 Work with a partner. Identify the items in the pictures.

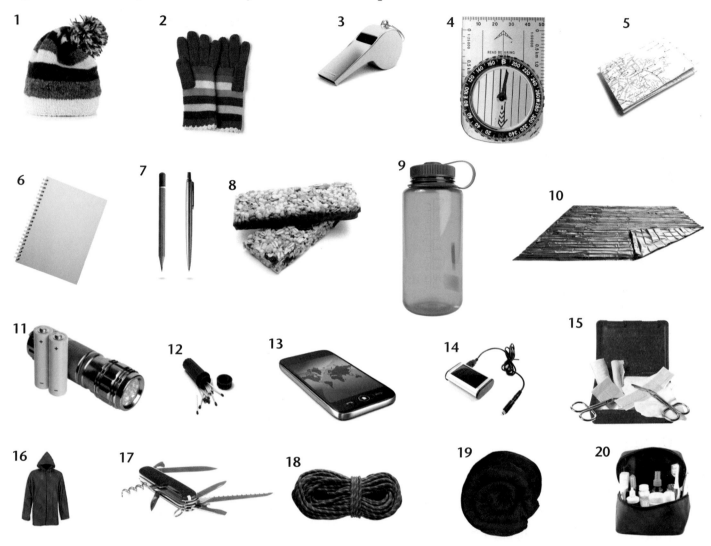

map	emergency food rations, e.g. energy bars	notebook	water bottle
hat	whistle	gloves	compass
solar phone recharger	waterproof jacket or poncho	first-aid kit: plasters, antiseptic wipes, bandages	multi-tool (knife, screwdriver, tin opener)
space blanket	waterproof matches	torch plus spare batteries	mobile phone
sleeping bag	washing kit	rope	pen & pencil

2 Explain why you need each item.

> You need a solar phone recharger to recharge your phone.

> You need a first-aid kit in case you injure yourself.

Language tip

You can use *in case* to talk about possibility.

*You need a first-aid kit **in case** you injure yourself.* = You need a first aid kit. You might injure yourself.

3 Work in pairs. Talk about what you need for a day's expedition. Make a list.

Project: Plan a day's expedition

4 **Work in groups of four.**

- You're going to go on a day's walk in an unfamiliar area.
- The walk is going to take eight hours.
- You will be walking in a place where there are no towns or villages.
- You will be in groups of four.
- You each have a rucksack measuring 40 cm × 25 cm.
- You need to take a survival kit in case you have problems.

1 Discuss these questions.
  1 Where are you going to walk?
  2 What problems might you have?
  3 What are you going to put in your rucksack? (Don't make your rucksack too heavy! You've got to carry it all day.)

2 Write a plan for your walk. Include the following:
  - Start time and place
  - Route
  - List of things to take and reasons for taking them.

3 Present your plan to the rest of the class and answer any questions.

Travel/Autobiography

In 1985, Joe Simpson and Simon Yates were the first mountaineers to climb the West Face of the Siula Grande, a mountain in the Andes, in Peru. Joe wrote a book about the experience.

1 Look at the cover of this book. Why did the publisher choose this picture? Does it make you want to read the book? Give your reasons.

2 Read the introduction and the extract. What pictures do you have in your mind as you read?

Joe and Simon reached the top of the mountain on the third day of their climb, but then began the difficult journey back down. Joe fell and broke his leg. Simon tried to help Joe by lowering him on a rope, but when he accidentally lowered him over a cliff, Joe was left hanging in mid-air….

Touching the Void

Above me the rope sawed through the cliff edge, dislodging chunks of crusty ice. I stared at it stretching into the darkness above. Cold had long since won its battle. There was no feeling in my arms and legs. Everything slowed and softened. Thoughts became idle questions, never answered. I accepted that I was to die. There was no alternative. It caused me no dreadful fear. I was numb with cold and felt no pain; so senselessly cold   5
that I craved sleep and cared nothing for the consequences. It would be a dreamless sleep. Reality had become a nightmare, and sleep beckoned insistently; a black hole calling me, pain-free, lost in time, like death.

My torch beam died. The cold had killed the batteries. I saw stars in a dark gap above me. Stars, or lights in my head. The storm was over. The stars were good to see. I was glad to see   10
them again. Old friends come back. They seemed far away; further than I'd ever seen them before. And bright: you'd think them gemstones hanging there, floating in the air above. Some moved, little winking moves, on and off, on and off, floating the brightest sparks of light down to me.

Then, what I had waited for pounced on me. The stars went out, and I fell. Like   15
something come alive, the rope lashed violently against my face and I fell silently, endlessly into nothingness, as if dreaming or falling. I fell fast, faster than thought, and my stomach protested at the swooping speed of it. I swept down, and from far above I saw myself falling and felt nothing. No thoughts, and all fears gone away. So this is it!

Touching the Void by Joe Simpson,
E-book published by Direct Authors
Vintage, 1998

sawed *(line 1)* moved like a saw (a tool used for cutting wood)

dislodging *(line 1)* moving something away from a fixed position

crusty *(line 1)* like the outside of a loaf of bread

stared *(line 1)* looked at for a long time

idle *(line 3)* not serious, without any purpose

dreadful *(line 5)* very bad or unpleasant

numb *(line 5)* having lost all feeling

craved *(line 6)* wanted very much

beckoned *(line 7)* made a sign that asks someone / something to come closer

beam *(line 9)* a line of light shining from a lamp

gemstones *(line 12)* jewels, beautiful stones that have been cut into special shapes

floating *(line 12)* moving gently through the air

winking *(line 13)* opening and closing one eye quickly

pounced *(line 15)* suddenly moved forward to attack, like a cat with mouse

lashed *(line 16)* hit with a whip

swooping *(line 18)* moving suddenly down through the air

swept *(line 18)* moved quickly

3 Read the extract again and answer the questions.

1 What does the first paragraph tell you about Joe's attitude towards his situation?

2 In the second paragraph, why is Joe happy to see the stars?

3 In the third paragraph, what do we learn about how Joe feels?

4 What is the meaning of the last sentence: "So this is it!"

4 Answer these questions about the style of the extract.

1 Look at the following phrases. The author could have left out the adjectives and adverbs. Why did he use them?

Adjectives	Adverbs
crusty ice *(line 1)*	beckoned insistently *(line 7)*
dreadful fear *(line 5)*	lashed violently *(line 16)*
swooping speed *(line 18)*	

2 How many times does the author use the word *cold*? What is the effect of this? Where does he use the technique of 'personification' (showing a thing or something abstract as a person)?

3 Is the language of the extract plain and simple, or is it colourful and poetic? Give examples.

5 Work in groups. Discuss these questions.

1 Does this extract give you a sense of what it was like for Joe in this situation? How does it make you feel?

2 Does the author make you feel that you want to read more?

133

Review of Units 15–16

Vocabulary

Natural disasters

1 Match the words to the definitions.

1 wildfire
2 earthquake
3 flood
4 hurricane
5 drought
6 famine

a a long period of time when there is little or no rain and crops die
b a sudden movement of the earth's surface, often causing a lot of damage
c a violent storm with very strong winds
d when very heavy rain causes rivers to burst their banks
e when people have little or no food and some of them die
f a fire that starts in an area of countryside and burns very quickly

Survival kit

2 Match the words to make compound nouns.

1 first-aid
2 energy
3 water
4 space
5 waterproof
6 solar
7 antiseptic
8 tin

a bars
b blanket
c bottle
d kit
e matches
f opener
g phone recharger
h wipes

3 Complete these sentences using the compound nouns from Exercise 2 and *in case* or *to*.

1 <u>You need a water bottle to</u> carry water, so that you don't get dehydrated.
2 _____ keep you warm in an emergency.
3 _____ keep your phone charged.
4 _____ light a fire in the rain.
5 _____ open cans of food.
6 _____ you cut yourself and need to clean the area of the cut.
7 _____ you injure yourself.
8 _____ you have no food left and you're hungry.

Use of English

4 Rewrite these sentences using the present perfect passive. Use *by* where necessary.

1 They've collected a lot of money for the charity appeal.
   A lot of money has been collected for the charity appeal.
2 International charities have sent emergency food rations.
   Emergency food rations ...
3 People have given blankets, sleeping bags and warm jackets.
4 They've sent a hospital ship.
5 Volunteer medical teams have treated people.
6 The army has supplied clean water.

5 Rewrite the sentences using *despite* or *in spite of*.

1 The walkers had a compass, but they got lost.
   Despite / In spite of having a compass, the walkers got lost.
2 The weather was really terrible, but we managed to reach the camp before dark.

Despite / In spite of the terrible weather, we managed to reach the camp before dark.

3 We had a sat nav in the car, but we ended up in the middle of a field.

4 I wore a thick jacket, a hat and gloves, but I was cold.

5 The farmers collected water during the rainy season, but they ran out of water in the dry season.

6 There was a flood, but the crops and the animals survived.

7 The firefighters dropped water from planes, but they couldn't stop the fire spreading.

8 The miners were trapped underground for several weeks, but they kept their spirits up.

6 Complete the sentences with *mustn't* or *don't have to.*

1 Today is the last day of term, so I ___ get up early tomorrow.

2 The coach leaves at 8.30, so you ___ be late.

3 You ___ be tall to be a good tennis player.

4 This is a test, so you ___ look at the answers.

5 We've got a week to do our project, so we ___ finish it tonight.

6 She's got such a good memory that she ___ do any revision for exams.

7 Make adverbs and comparative adverbs from these adjectives. Then use them to complete the sentences below.

Adjective	Adverb	Comparative adverb
good	well	better
bad		
careful		
clear		
quick		
safe		

1 You can cross the road much <u>more safely</u> if you use the pedestrian crossing.

2 My friend's a good singer. She sings much ___ than I do.

3 My younger brother says he could get home much ___ ___ if he took his skateboard to school.

4 I've skied much ___ ___ since I nearly went down a black run by mistake!

5 I did badly in the Maths test but I did much ___ in the exam. I only got two out of twenty.

6 You need to speak much ___ ___ when you're talking to someone who doesn't speak your language well.

General knowledge quiz

8 Work with a partner. Ask and answer the questions.

1 What do you call the area of land directly over the centre of an earthquake?

2 What is the name of the imaginary line around the earth that is the same distance from the North Pole and the South Pole?

3 For a fire to burn, three things are necessary: a heat source (such as a match or lightning), fuel and which gas?

4 What kind of organisation is ActionAid?

5 Name three countries in East Africa.

6 In which South American country is Lima?

7 Where are the Comoros Islands?

8 The collapse of a gold and copper mine became international news in 2010. Where was the mine? How many miners were trapped? How many survived?

9 What is this race called?

10 What is 'apple bobbing'?

135

- **Topics** Summer holidays; summer camps and outdoor activities; staying in a hotel
- **Use of English** Past modals; indirect and embedded questions

Summer holidays

- What's your favourite kind of summer holiday?

Vocabulary

1 Use a word from each column to make compound nouns to describe the holiday items above.

1	first-aid	**a**	chair
2	sun	**b**	box
3	insect	**c**	kit
4	sun	**d**	repellent
5	cool	**e**	cream
6	picnic	**f**	hat
7	folding	**g**	basket

2 What kind of holiday would you be going on if you took everything from Exercise 1?

3 Complete the opinions about holidays with words from the box.

| bored | fun | nice | relaxed | sociable | uncomfortable |

I think camping holidays are the best because you spend a lot of time outside in the fresh air. It's so ....[1] to be outside after spending a lot of time inside during the school term. The other thing is that you can play table tennis and football, you can go swimming, that kind of thing. You never get ....[2].

Elisabet

Sea, sun and sand — what more do you need? When you spend all day on the beach and in the sea you feel really ....[5]. And you can lie under a sun shade and read a book or text your friends. It can be quite ....[6] because it's easy to make new friends there.

Eugenia

Camping holidays aren't really for me. You get bitten by insects. It's too hot at night and there might be a spider in your sleeping bag. It's very ....[3] and there could be wolves or bears prowling around. And barbecues aren't much ....[4] because Dad always burns the food. I'd rather stay at home.

Martin

4 Read the texts again and answer the questions.
1 Which two people would get on well: Elisabet, Martin, Eugenia?
2 Who likes to take it easy on holiday?
3 Which of the people would you describe as
  • cautious?
  • active?
  • extrovert?
4 Choose one item from Exercise 1 for each person (Elisabet, Martin and Eugenia) to take on holiday. Give reasons for your choice.

Speaking

5 Work with a partner. Say which opinion in Exercise 3 you agree with and why. If you don't agree with any of them, talk about the kind of summer holiday you like or don't like.

Summer camp in Japan

- Do you think summer camps for children and teenagers are a good idea?

Vocabulary

1 Read the description of the summer camp on the website. Make a list of the phrases which create a positive picture. (Use a dictionary to help you if you're not sure of the meaning.)

the ultimate get-away, serious fun, ...

Our camps are the ultimate get-away for children who are keen to have some serious fun while experiencing a fantastic summer programme in Japan, based in a natural setting at beautiful Lake Aokiko (15 minutes from Hakuba and one of Japan's purest lakes).

Campers stay at Hotel Blue Lake, equipped with comfortable futons, *onsens* (hot baths) and buffet dinner/breakfast accommodating all dietary needs. The Extreme camp also includes a night camping in tents on the top of the hills overlooking Hakuba village with an amazing view of the Northern Alps. Activities vary, depending on the camp chosen, and include outdoor games, swimming, craft, campfires, cook-outs, canoeing, hiking, mountain-biking, canyoning and more.

SUMMER CAMP SCHEDULE
Day 1
- Meet and travel
- Campsite and team orientation/introductions
- Fun activity
- Welcome campfire

Day 2
- Swimming at Lake Aokiko
- Camp games
- Night canoe to see fireflies

Day 3
- Group 1: canoeing
- Group 2: raft building
- Evening activity

Day 4
- Group 1: raft building
- Group 2: canoeing
- Evening activity

Day 5
- Craft activity
- Closing ceremony
- Travel back to Tokyo

EXTREME CAMP SCHEDULE
Day 1
- Meet and travel
- Campsite and team orientation/introductions
- Spend the afternoon canoeing and swimming in beautiful Lake Aokiko
- Welcome campfire

Day 2
- Swimming and canoeing at Lake Aokiko
- Night canoe to see fireflies

Day 3
- Canyoning
- High ropes
- Evening activity

Day 4
- Nature craft
- Mountain biking and overnight camp
- Campfire

Day 5
- Camp breakfast
- Mountain biking
- Closing ceremony
- Travel back to Tokyo

Text from: www.evergreen-hakuba.com

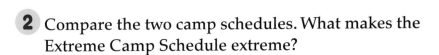

2 Compare the two camp schedules. What makes the Extreme Camp Schedule extreme?

Speaking

3 Work with a partner. Which camp schedule do you prefer? Give your reasons.

4 Read the following message and answer the questions.

1 Who enjoyed her holiday and who didn't?

2 What sort of holiday did each of them go on?

New Message	
To:	Hi Misako,
Message:	Sorry to hear you didn't enjoy your holiday at the beach. I know what you mean, beach holidays can be boring! You should have come with us. You could have done mountain biking and canoeing. You would have learned to build a shelter out of wood and cook on a campfire. You wouldn't have been bored! Anyway, maybe you can come with us next year.
	See you at school on Monday.
	Ariya

Send **Cancel**

5 Complete the sentences using past modals and the verbs in brackets.

1 I didn't know you were free last Saturday. We <u>could have gone</u> bowling. (*go*)

2 You've been bitten. You _____ some insect repellent. (*put on*)

3 We _____ the burgers on the campfire for so long. They were all burnt! (*not leave*)

4 The music was so good at the party that I _____ all night. (*dance*)

5 My stomach hurts. I _____ so much cake! (*not eat*)

6 You _____ the programme about extreme sports. You _____ it. (*watch, enjoy*)

Writing

6 Write a letter or a message to a friend explaining why you wish they had come on a recent trip or holiday with you. Use Ariya's message in Exercise 4 as a model.

You should have come with us to meet my cousins. You would have got on really well with them. We could have ...

Use of English: Past modals

Use *should have / shouldn't have* + past participle to express regret or criticism.

You should have come with us.
= I'm sorry you didn't come with us. / I wish you had come with us.

Remember that you can use *could have* and *would have* + past participle to talk about things that were possible, but did not happen.

If you had come with us, ...

you could have done mountain biking and canoeing;

you would have learned to build a shelter out of wood and cook on a campfire;

you wouldn't have been bored.

A room with a view

- What's good about staying in a hostel or a hotel on holiday? Are there any disadvantages?

Listening 31

1 Listen to the dialogue and answer the questions.

1 Where does it take place?
2 How would you describe the attitude of the manager?
- helpful / unhelpful
- friendly / unfriendly
- polite / impolite

Reading

2 Read the dialogue. Why is the guest confused about the time breakfast is served?

Guest: *Could you tell me what time breakfast is, please?*

Manager: *Yes, I could.*

Guest: *Well, umm, what time is it?*

Manager: *Breakfast is from 7 till 10, but you need to tell me what time you want it.*

Guest: *Umm, well could we have it at 7.30 tomorrow?*

Manager: *No.*

Guest: *But you just said …*

Manager: *Not on a Sunday. It starts at 8 o'clock on a Sunday.*

Guest: *Well, 8 o'clock's fine. Do you know if there's a bus into town this morning?*

Manager: *Yes, I do.*

Guest: *Well, is there a bus into town?*

Manager: *Oh, just look at the timetable. There's one in your room. Now, I wonder if you'd mind letting me get on with my work. Can't you see that I'm busy? The hostel is full this weekend and I've got a lot to do.*

3 Rewrite these questions as indirect/embedded questions.

1 What's the time?
I wonder _what the time is_.

2 Where is the tourist information office?
Can you tell me _____?

3 Where can I get a map?
Could you tell me _____?

4 Where did I put my key?
I can't remember _____.

5 Is there a table tennis table?
I wonder _____.

6 Is breakfast included in the price of the room?
Do you know _____?

Listening (32)

4 Listen to these conversations. What does each guest want?

5 Read the information about Sea View Hostel and listen again. Who is right in each situation, the guest or the hostel manager?

Project: Write a sketch

6 Work in groups. Write a sketch set in the Sea View Hostel.

Setting: The Sea View Hostel
Characters: The manager
Guests

1 Try out some ideas for your script. Improvise some dialogues.
2 Note down the lines that work well, especially the ones that are funny.
3 Write a full script which includes the lines you've written.
4 Ask your teacher to check your script.
5 Decide who is going to play each character.
6 Rehearse your sketch. Then perform it in front of the class.

Use of English: Indirect and embedded questions

To ask for information and to make questions more polite, we often start with a phrase like *Do you know ...?* or *Could you tell me ...?*

Could you tell me what time breakfast is please?

Notice that the word order is different from the word order in a simple question.

What time is breakfast, please?

Could you tell me what time breakfast is, please?

You don't use the auxiliaries *do*, *does* or *did* in embedded questions.

What time do you want it?

You need to tell me what time you want it. (NOT *You need to tell me what time do you want it.*)

With *Yes / No* questions, use *if* or *whether*.

Is there a bus into town?

Do you know if / whether there is a bus into town?

SEA VIEW HOSTEL

Enjoy our comfortable rooms, all of which have wonderful views.

Supper served from 6.30 to 8.00.

Free wifi for our guests.

Don't worry if you've forgotten your toothpaste, toothbrush, etc. Just call reception – you can buy them there.

18 Using English

- **Topics** Performing on stage; the story of Midas; writing and performing scenes from a play
- **Use of English** Reported speech (revision): statements, questions and commands; punctuation: full stops and commas

King Midas

Reading

1 Read the poster. What is it for? What is *The Golden Touch*?

The Golden Touch

We're auditioning for **The Golden Touch**, based on the story of King Midas.

If you're interested in auditioning for a part, contact us and we'll send you details and an audition script.

Auditions will be held on 11th and 12th June.

Listening 33

2 Listen to two actors at the auditions. Who sounds more confident, Sarah or Tom?

3 Read what Sarah and Tom said after the auditions. Who said what?

1 They asked me if I knew the story.   *Sarah*
2 I said I could sing and dance.
3 I said I was playing the part of a princess at my local theatre.
4 They asked me what I thought of the story of Midas.
5 I told them I'd been at stage school since I was six.
6 They asked me if I had had a main part in a play before.
7 They asked me if I would be available in September.
8 When I started to read, they told me to speak up.

142

Use of English: Reported speech (revision): statements, questions and commands

When we tell people what someone said, we usually change the tense of the verb because what they said was in the past.

"I can sing and dance." → *I told them I could sing and dance. / She said she could sing and dance.*

"I was in Alice in Wonderland." → *I told them I'd been in Alice in Wonderland. / He said he'd been in Alice in Wonderland.*

When you report questions that begin with a question word, change the tense and leave out *do / does / did.*

"What do you think of the story of Midas?" → *The director asked me what I thought of the story of Midas.*

When you report Yes / No questions, use *if,* change the tense and leave out *do / does / did.*

"Do you know the story?" → *He asked me if I knew the story.*

When you report a command, use this structure: *ask / tell* someone *to* do something.

"Speak up a bit." → *He told me to speak up a bit.*

4 What were the original statements and questions that Sarah and Tom reported in Exercise 3?

<u>**Reported speech**</u>

1 They asked me if I knew the story.

<u>**Direct speech (original statement / question)**</u>

"Do you know the story?"

5 Report the statements and questions.

1 "I'm in a play at my local theatre."
Sarah said she *was in a play at her local theatre.*

2 "Are you in anything at the moment?"
The director asked Sarah

_____ .

3 "Imagine you're alone in your palace."
The stage manager told Tom

_____ .

4 "I can't hear you."
The director told Tom that

_____ .

5 "I'm looking forward to reading the story."
Tom said he _____ .

Speaking

6 Work with a partner. Have a conversation about the theatre using these questions.

1 Have you ever been to the theatre? (What did you see?)
2 Are you good at acting?
3 Do you like reading aloud in class?
4 Can you sing and dance?
5 Which do you prefer, the theatre or the cinema?

The story of Midas

Which stories do you remember from your childhood? Why do you remember them?

Midas

Once upon a time, there was a king called Midas. He ruled over the ancient kingdom of Phrygia. One day, two farm workers brought an old man to him. His name was Silenus. He had lost his way
5 and was wandering in the countryside when they found him.

Midas recognised the old man as a wise and famous teacher. He welcomed him to his court and for ten days and nights, he entertained him at his
10 palace. In return for Midas's generous hospitality, Silenus told him many stories.

When Silenus was fit and strong again, Midas took him back to his home in Lydia, a neighbouring kingdom. There, Silenus was reunited with one of
15 his young students, Dionysus.

Dionysus was so pleased to see his teacher that he asked Midas to choose a gift – anything he wanted. Midas thought for a while and then asked Dionysus if he could have the power to turn everything that
20 he touched to gold. Dionysus reluctantly agreed. He wished that Midas had asked for something better, but there was nothing he could do.

Midas decided to test his new gift immediately. He touched the branch of a tree and he couldn't
25 believe his eyes when it turned to gold. He picked up a stone. It too turned to gold. Then he picked an apple from a tree and held it in his hand. It became a golden apple. Even when he washed his hands in clear water, the water turned to liquid gold. Midas
30 was delighted. He would be the richest man in the world.

Midas went home to his palace. He was hungry after the journey so he asked his servants to bring him some food and something to drink. But when
35 he touched a piece of bread, it became solid gold and he couldn't eat it. He tried to eat some meat, but as soon as his teeth touched it, it too turned into gold. Even water turned to liquid gold as he drank it.

40 Midas was beginning to realise that he had made a terrible mistake. At that moment, his daughter Aurelia came into the room. Her father was looking very anxious so she asked him what was wrong. When he didn't answer, she ran towards him and
45 put her arms around him. He watched in horror as his beautiful daughter turned into a golden statue. If only he hadn't asked for the golden touch! The king was in despair. He didn't know what to do. He couldn't eat or drink and he had lost his only
50 daughter.

The following day, Dionysus came to see how Midas was enjoying his gift. Midas told him that he had wanted to be the richest man in the world but in fact, he was the poorest. He said he had lost
55 what was most precious to him.

Dionysus asked Midas which he would rather have, a cup of cold water or the golden touch. Midas asked for a cup of water. Dionysus then asked him to choose between a piece of bread
60 and the golden touch. Midas replied that he would much rather have a simple piece of bread. Finally, Dionysus asked him if he wanted to have his daughter back or to have all the gold in the world. "My daughter, my daughter, my beautiful child!"
65 cried Midas.

Dionysus felt sorry for Midas and he knew that the king had learned a useful lesson. So he told Midas to go to the source of the River Pactolus to wash away his crime in its waters.

70 Midas did as Dionysus said. His power to change things into gold passed from him into the river. Midas left his grand palace and went to live a simple, happy life in the country with his daughter.

Reading

1 Read the story of Midas on page 144. Why did Ovid include it in *Metamorphoses*?

2 Work with a partner. Take turns to ask and answer the questions.

1 Who were Midas, Silenus and Dionysus?
2 How did Silenus get to Midas's palace?
3 How did Midas treat Silenus?
4 Why did Dionysus reward Midas?
5 What was Midas's wish?
6 How did Midas's view of the golden touch change?
7 What was the useful lesson that Midas had learned?
8 How did Midas lose the golden touch?

3 Put the commas and full stops in this paragraph. Remember to put capital letters at the start of sentences. Who is speaking here?

"i had a wonderful time at Midas's palace he was very kind to me when we returned to Lydia my student Dionysus asked Midas what he wanted as a gift Midas asked for the power to turn everything he touched to gold Dionysus didn't think it was a good idea although Midas is not a greedy man he wanted to be the richest man in the world when he turned his daughter into a gold statue his dream turned into a nightmare."

Speaking

4 Work with a partner. Answer the questions.

1 Which of these sayings relate to the story of Midas?
- A fool and his money are soon parted.
- Money isn't everything.
- All that glitters isn't gold.
- The best things in life are free.
- Money can't buy happiness.
- Be careful what you wish for.

2 If you could have any wish, what would you wish for?

Use of English: Punctuation – full stops and commas

A sentence is a group of words, usually containing a verb, which expresses a complete idea. We use a full stop at the end of a sentence. Sentences always start with a capital letter.

Once upon a time there was a king called Midas. He ruled over the ancient kingdom of Phrygia. (These are two complete ideas. You cannot use a comma to separate them.)

Commas separate clauses within a sentence.

In return for Midas's generous hospitality, Silenus told him many stories.

When Silenus was fit and strong again, Midas took him back to his home.

The performance

Project: *The Golden Touch* – a play about King Midas

You are going to write a play based on the story of Midas.

1 There are four main characters – **King Midas, Silenus, Dionysus** and **Aurelia** – and a **narrator**. There are four or more minor characters (**farm workers** and **servants**). You also need to have a **stage manager** and a **props manager**.
2 Divide the class into two groups. Each group writes their own version of the play.
3 There are six scenes in the play. The outline of each scene is given on page 147.
4 Write the dialogue for each scene. Refer back to the story on page 144.
5 Your teacher will check your script.

If you decide to perform your play, read the following.

1 You will need these props:

a small branch from a tree

a stone

an apple

water in a bowl for Midas to wash his hands in

a tray with something to eat and something to drink on it

2 Choose the parts you're going to play. Remember you also need a stage manager and a props manager.
3 Rehearse the play, scene by scene. Speak clearly and slowly. Use movement and facial expressions to help your audience understand what you are saying. Your teacher will check your pronunciation.
4 Give a performance of *The Golden Touch*.

The Golden Touch

> Describe where the scene takes place.

Scene 1 *The countryside near Midas's palace; Midas's palace*

> List the characters appearing in this scene.

NARRATOR, TWO FARM WORKERS, MIDAS, SILENUS

NARRATOR: Once upon a time, there was a king called Midas. He ruled over the ancient kingdom of Phrygia. One day, two farm workers brought an old man to him. His name was Silenus. He had lost his way and was wandering in the countryside when they found him.

> Give stage directions.

Silenus is wandering round, looking lost.

SILENUS: Where am I? I'm lost. Please help me! I'm an old man and I'm tired. I don't know where I am.

Enter two farm workers.

FARM WORKER 1: Look. There's an old man over there. He's lost.

FARM WORKER 2: ...

[Write your dialogue based on lines 1–11 on page 144.]

Scene 2 *Lydia*

NARRATOR, MIDAS, SILENUS AND DIONYSUS

NARRATOR: When Silenus was fit and strong again, Midas took him back to his home in Lydia, a neighbouring kingdom. There Silenus was reunited with one of his young students, Dionysus.

MIDAS: Here we are. Now, where is Dionysus?

[Write your dialogue based on lines 12–22 on page 144.]

Scene 3 *On the road between Lydia and Phrygia.*

NARRATOR, MIDAS

NARRATOR: Midas decided to test his new gift immediately.

MIDAS: ...

[Write your dialogue based on lines 23–31 on page 144.]

Scene 4 *Midas's palace*

MIDAS, TWO SERVANTS, AURELIA (MIDAS'S DAUGHTER)

MIDAS: I'm hungry and thirsty. Bring me ...

[Write your dialogue based on lines 32–50 on page 144.]

Scene 5 *Midas's palace*

DIONYSUS, MIDAS, AURELIA (AS A STATUE)

DIONYSUS: Midas, how are you? Are you enjoying your gift?

[Write your dialogue based on lines 51–65 on page 144.]

Scene 6 *Near the source of the River Pactolus*

NARRATOR, DIONYSUS, MIDAS, AURELIA (AS HERSELF)

NARRATOR: Dionysus felt sorry for Midas and he knew that the king had learned a useful lesson.

[Write your dialogue based on lines 66–73 on page 144.]

NARRATOR: And they lived happily ever after!

The End

Fiction

The Village by the Sea

Anita Desai was born and educated in India. She's written novels, short stories and books for children.

1 Look at the illustration on the cover of the book. What does it show?

2 This is the opening of Chapter 1 of *The Village by the Sea*. What impression is the author trying to give?

The Village by the Sea

When Lila went out on the beach it was so early in the morning that there was no one else there. The sand was washed clean by last night's tide and no one had walked on it except the birds
5 that fished along the coast – gulls, curlews and sandpipers. She walked down to the sea with the small basket she carried on the flat of her hand, filled with flowers she had plucked from the garden around their house – scarlet hibiscus
10 blooms, sweet-smelling spider lilies and bright butter-yellow allamanda flowers.

When she came to the edge of the sea, she lifted the folds of her sari and tucked them up at her waist, then waded out into the
15 waves that came rushing over her feet and swirling about her ankles in creamy foam. She waded in till she came to a cluster of three rocks. One of them was daubed with red and white powder. It was the sacred rock, a kind
20 of temple in the sea. At high tide it would be inundated but now, at low tide, it could be freshly consecrated. Lila took the flowers from her basket and scattered them about the rock, then folded her hands and bowed.

25 Just then the sun lifted up over the coconut palms in a line along the beach and sent long slanting rays over the silvery sand to touch her on the back of her head. Enjoying their warmth, she stayed bowed for a little
30 while, her feet still in the cold, whispering waves. The sun lit up the pink and mauve waves with sparkles. Far out, stretched along the horizon, was the fishing fleet that had been out all night, the sails like white wings,
35 or fins, lifting out of the sea. They were anchored and still: they would not return before sundown.

by Anita Desai

gull

curlew

sandpiper

coconut palm (tree)

hibiscus flowers

spider lilies

allamanda flowers

the flat of her hand (line 7–8) her hand turned upwards and stretched out

plucked (a flower) (line 8) picked (a word used in books, but not usually in conversation)

tucked (line 13) pushed (the edge of a piece of cloth) into a small space

waded (line 14) walked through water

swirling (line 16) moving around and around quickly

cluster (line 17) a group of similar things that are close together

daubed (line 18) painted quickly, without care

consecrated (line 22) made holy

scattered (line 23) spread over a wide area

slanting (line 27) at an angle

sparkles (line 32) small reflections of light

stretched (line 32) spread out

anchored (line 36) when a boat is stopped from moving by an anchor (a heavy metal object)

3 **Answer these questions about the vocabulary the author uses.**

1 How many words in the extract can you find to do with the natural world?

Landscape	Sea	Animals	Plants and trees
beach	tide		

2 How many words for colours can you find?
scarlet, ...

3 Find two compound adjectives in the extract.

4 Look at these adjectives + nouns. Why do you think the author chose these particular adjectives?
whispering waves (line 30)
silvery sand (line 27)
creamy foam (line 16)

5 The five senses are: sight, sound, touch, taste and smell. Which ones does the author appeal to in this extract?

4 **Work with a partner. What impression do you get of life in this place?**

5 **Write a description of an early-morning visit to a beautiful place near where you live, as if for the opening chapter of a story.**

Review of Units 17–18

Vocabulary

Summer holidays

1 Write the names of the items using the words on the beach umbrella. Clue: they're all compound nouns.

Use of English

2 Complete the sentences with the correct words.

uncomfortable   fun   bored   relaxed   sociable

1 I'm never _____ on a beach holiday because I spend all day swimming, surfing and windsurfing.

2 Summer holidays are great because you don't have anything to worry about. You feel very _____ .

3 My brother always makes new friends on holiday. He's very _____ .

4 My mum and dad don't like camping. They say it's too _____ .

5 It's _____ to cook over a campfire because it's different and because you're outside.

3 Rewrite the following sentences.

Use *should have / shouldn't have*

1 I wish we'd gone on the night canoeing trip to see the fireflies.

   We should have gone on the night canoeing trip to see the fireflies.

2 I wish we hadn't sat in the sun without putting sun cream on.

3 It's a pity we didn't go on the three-day camping holiday.

Use *could have / couldn't have*

4 Raft building was on the list of activities, but we didn't do it.

   We could have done raft building. It was on the list of activities.

5 It wasn't possible to phone you because there was no mobile phone signal.

6 There was paella on the menu at the café yesterday, but we didn't have it.

4 Make these questions more polite by using *Could you tell me ...?* or *Do you know ...?* Then look at the signs and write the answers.

1 What time does the shop close?

   –*Could you tell me what time the shop closes?*
   –*Yes, it closes at 10 o'clock in the evening.*

2 What time does the café open?
3 Is there a bus stop near here?
4 Can you hire mountain bikes?
5 Is there a table tennis area?
6 Is it OK to bring pets to the campsite?

General knowledge quiz

5 Work with a partner. Ask and answer the questions.

1 What is this: an onsen, a futon or a kimono? In which country would you find it?
2 Where is Lake Aokiko?
   a New Zealand   b Japan   c Hawaii
3 He was a king in a story and everything he touched turned to gold. Who was he?
4 Who wrote the poem *Metamorphoses*?
5 What does the word *metamorphosis* mean?
6 Complete these sayings:
   * A _____ and his money are soon parted.
   * All that glitters isn't _____.
   * _____ can't buy happiness.
7 Who or what was Phrygia?
   a a river   b an ancient kingdom
   c a wise old man
8 Who or what is Pactolus?
   a a river   b a country
   c a philosopher
9 What do you call the test that actors do to be selected for a part in a play?
10 What does a narrator do in a play or a film?

Acknowledgements

The authors and publishers would like to thank the following for their contribution to the development of Stage 8:

Series Editor: Peter Lucantoni; Development Editor: Sian Mavor; Project Manager: Charlotte al-Qadi; Reviewers: Nahla El Geyoushi; Lois Hopkins, MA Publishing; Ana Pérez Moreno, Licentiate in English Language and in Education; Claire Olmez, BEd, MA ELT; Mary Spratt.

Cover artwork: saint horant daniel/Shutterstock

The authors and publishers acknowledge the following sources of copyright material and are grateful for the permissions granted. While every effort has been made, it has not always been possible to identify the sources of all the material used, or to trace all copyright holders. If any omissions are brought to our notice, we will be happy to include the appropriate acknowledgements on reprinting.

p. 21 excerpt from *City of the Beasts* (original title *La ciudad de las bestias*) by Isabel Allende, HarperCollins 2002, © 2002 Isabel Allende, English translation copyright © 2002 HarperCollins Publishers, Inc., reproduced by permission of HarperCollins Publishers and Agencia Literaria Carmen Balcells. p. 32 excerpt and illustration from *Into the Unknown* by Stewart Ross, text © 2011 by Stewart Ross, illustrations © 2011 by Stephen Biesty, reproduced by permission of Walker Books Ltd. London SE11 5HJ, www.walker.co.uk. p. 33 audio content relating to exercise 'Listening 8' on this page is from *Into the Unknown* by Stewart Ross, text copyright © Stewart Ross, reproduced by permission of Walker Books Ltd. London SE11 5HJ. p. 37 excerpt from *Chike and the River* by Chunua Achebe, 1996, © Cambridge University Press 1966, reproduced by permission; pp. 40, 41 illustrations from *Cambridge School Dictionary* 2008 © Cambridge University Press 2008, reproduced by permission; p. 48 adapted excerpts from 'Jumping through hoops: life as a circus performer' by Helen McGurk, from *News Letter* (www.newsletter. co.uk), reproduced by permission; p. 53 excerpt from *Bend it Like Beckham* by Narinder Dhami (Copyright © Narinder Dhami) is reproduced by permission of United Agents (www.unitedagents.co.uk) on behalf of Narinder Dhami; p. 69 excerpt from *The Whale Rider* by Witi Ihimaera, reproduced by permission of Penguin NZ; p. 84 'Where I Come From' by Elizabeth Brewster is reprinted from *Selected Brewster* by permission of Oberon Press, Canada; p. 101 excerpt from *Rickshaw Girl*, text copyright © 2003 by Mitali Perkins, reproduced by permission of Charlesbridge Publishing, Inc., all rights reserved; p. 116 excerpt from *Coming to England* by Floella Benjamin, text © 1995 Floella Benjamin, reproduced by permission of Walker Books Ltd. London SE11 5HJ; p. 122 case study from 'Free teaching resources: Disasters and Emergencies - East Africa Drought' from www.actionaid.org.uk, reproduced by permission of ActionAid UK. p. 126 excerpt adapted from article 'The children who survive plane crashes' by Nigel Farndale in The Telegraph, July 2009, © Telegraph News & Media ltd 2009, reproduced by permission; p. 132 excerpt from *Touching the Void* by Joe Simpson, Vintage 1998, E-book published by Direct Authors, reproduced by permission of Direct Authors. p.138 excerpts from 'English Summer Camps in Hakuba, Japan' and 'Specific Camp Schedules' from www.evergreen-hakuba.com, reproduced by permission of the Evergreen Outdoor Center; p. 148 excerpt from *The Village by the Sea* by Anita Desai, copyright © Anita Desai 1982, reproduced by permission of the author c/o Rogers, Coleridge & White Ltd., 20 Powis Mews, London W11 1NJ.

Thanks to the following for permission to reproduce images:

p. 21 cover art of *City of the Beasts* by Isabel Allende, copyright © 2002 Cliff Nielsen, by permission of HarperCollins Publishers; p. 126 cover of *When I Fell from the Sky* by Juliane Koepcke by permission of Nicholas Brealey Publishing; p. 132 cover of *Touching the Void* by Joe Simpson by permission of Direct Authors; p. 148 cover of *The Village by the Sea* by Anita Desai (Penguin Books 1984, 1988, 1992, 2001), copyright © Anita Desai, 1982, by permission of Penguin Books Ltd;

Cover: ephotocorp/Alamy; unit headers: u1 Getty Images/ E+/Tuomas Kujansuu; u2 Thinkstock/iStock/Eduard Titov; u3 Alamy/Marvin Dembinsky Photo Associates; u4 Alamy/ Lordprice Collection; u5 Thinkstock/iStock/jokerproduction; u6 Thinkstock/iStock/Oleksiy Mark; u7 Thinkstock/Fuse; u8 Shutterstock.com/Scott E Read; u9 Alamy/Art Kowalsky; u11 Getty Images/E+/ranplett; u12 Getty Images/Photodisc/David Fischer; u13 Thinkstock/TongRo Images; u14 Thinkstock/ iStock/MaxRiesgo; u15 Shutterstock.com/Bruno Ismael Silva Alves; u16 Thinkstock/Stockbyte; u17 Thinkstock/ iStock/david franklin; u18 Mary Evans Picture Library/ ARTHUR RACKHAM; p. 8C: Getty Images/E+/ranplett; p. 10: Alamy/redbrickstock.com; p. 12: Thinkstock/Stockbyte/ Brand X Pictures; p. 16: Vectorfusionart/Shutterstock; p. 19B: Shutterstock.com/ockap; p. 24–25: Pyramids from the Island of Roda (oil on canvas), Dillon, Frank (1823–1909) / Private Collection / Photo ©The Maas Gallery, London / The Bridgeman Art Library; p. 25B: Shutterstock.com/Julian W; p. 28: Getty Images/AFP/MARTIN BERNETTI; pp. 29B, 39B: Alamy/John Warburton-Lee Photography; p. 30B: Getty Images/Time Life Pictures/Mansell/Time Life Pictures; p. 34: Standford Torus by Donald E Davis. Public Domain; p. 36–37: Getty Images/National Geographic/W. Robert Moore; p. 42T: Getty Images/Shaun Botterill; p. 42B: Getty Images/Francois Nel; p. 44 (drummer): Shutterstock.com/Telekhovskyi; p. 44 (trampoline): Thinkstock/iStock/herreid; p. 44 (karate): Thinkstock/iStock/Bela Tiberiu Attl; p. 44 (reading): Thinkstock/ Creatas/Creatas Images; p. 44 (guitar): Thinkstock/iStock/Igor Sokolov; p. 44 (singer):